RACING AT CRYSTAL PALACE

RACING AT
CRYSTAL PALACE

A history of motorsports at
London's own race circuit 1927–1972

PHILLIP PARFITT

MRP

MOTOR RACING PUBLICATIONS LIMITED
Unit 6, The Pilton Estate, 46 Pitlake, Croydon, CR0 3RA, England

This work is published with the assistance of the Michael Sedgwick Memorial Trust. Founded in memory of the famous motoring researcher and author Michael Sedgwick (1926–1983), the Trust is a registered charity to encourage new research and recording of motoring history. Suggestions for future projects, and donations, should be sent to the Honorary Secretary of the Michael Sedgwick Memorial Trust, c/o the John Montagu Building, Beaulieu, Hampshire, S04 7ZN, England

First published 1991

Write for a free complete catalogue of MRP books to Motor Racing Publications Ltd, Unit 6, the Pilton Estate, 46 Pitlake, Croydon CR0 3RA

British Library Cataloguing in Publication Data

Parfitt, Phillip
  Racing at Crystal Palace.
  I. Title
  796.7206842178

  ISBN 0-947981-38-1

Typeset by Ryburn Typesetting Ltd
Origination by Ryburn Reprographics, Halifax

Printed in Great Britain by
The Amadeus Press Limited, Huddersfield, West Yorkshire

Contents

Introduction

Being a 12-year-old who was interested in motor sports but too young to have my own transport was a bit of a disadvantage. Neither Brands Hatch nor Silverstone was within easy reach by public transport, but for anyone living in the South London area Crystal Palace was! So it was there, in 1965, that I attended my first motorcycle race meeting, emerging from the No 157 bus at the gates of the circuit. I remember mostly the noise, speed and smell of the machines as I watched fascinated from the terraces that surrounded the track. After that day, I attended virtually every car and bike meeting held at the Palace, and when the circuit closed in 1972 I felt as though I was losing an old friend.

Racing at the Palace always seemed close and exciting, and invariably there was an unmistakable Crystal Palace atmosphere, which was produced, no doubt, by the friendliness of the circuit itself. Since that first meeting I have visited many other circuits both at home and abroad, but have never experienced quite the same atmosphere.

When I started to attend Palace meetings I had no idea that the circuit had such a long and interesting history, but now I wish I had been around some 30 years earlier to witness the exploits of many of the famous names who won – and lost – at the Palace.

In my all-too-brief time as a Palace regular I watched from every vantage point in all weathers, and I acted as a marshal at some of the last events. I can honestly say I was never bored by the racing there and can still remember vividly many thrilling events. I am sure that many other enthusiasts will remember them, too, and I hope that the following pages will rekindle for them many memories of the Palace as well as serve as a tribute to the circuit in all its forms and to all who raced on it.

The Crystal Palace circuit is now part of racing history, but I am sure it will never be forgotten by those who raced, spectated or marshalled there. I hope that the story of how it all came about and how eventually it all came to an end will recapture a little bit of that special 'Palace atmosphere'.

Phillip Parfitt

Acknowledgements

I am grateful to many people who offered me valuable assistance during the research of this book. In particular I would like to record my thanks to Allan Tyler, a former circuit manager at Crystal Palace; Brian Woolley and Kim White, who allowed me access to the *Classic Motor Cycle* archives at the EMAP National headquarters in Peterborough; the staff of the Greater London Photographic Library; Sydney Offord and the ladies at the British Automobile Racing Club at Thruxton Circuit; and S C Walsh, of Holts Products, who tracked down important information on the Holts Trophy races. I am also indebted to Alan Burgess, of the British Kart Club; members of the Aston Martin Owners Club; Melvyn Harrison, of the Crystal Palace Foundation; and Lionel Crossley, a former Crystal Palace Speedway rider, whose own book about the team provided much of the information for the chapter on The Glaziers.

A number of professional photographers known to have been active during the Crystal Palace years, as well as owners of photographic archives, were approached and they responded with a wide selection of material, and in particular I would like to record my thanks to Geoffrey Goddard, David Hodges, Nick Nicholls, Fred Scatley, Chris Harvey and Peter Hull, while my publisher's own photographic archive also included work from Trevor Morgan and Peter Tempest.

Letters placed in the motor sporting press requesting Crystal Palace memorabilia suitable for reproduction brought a large response from enthusiasts and former Palace marshals and competitors. Many people who were complete strangers to me, and I to them, were kind enough to loan me valuable programmes, race reports and photographs, for which I am most grateful, and in many instances were pleased to share their memories of the Palace with me. Inevitably, the quality of the photography from these sources varied, but not the enthusiasm with which it was offered, and I am as appreciative of the efforts of those whose work had to be rejected as I am of those who will find at least one of their photographs reproduced on the following pages.

Not all of the photographic prints were clearly identified, and I apologise if there are any omissions from the following list of people who deserve my gratitude for their efforts to assist me in my task: D R Ansell, Guy Ashenden, W E Avory, J G Baldwin, Mrs A E Brace, Alan Broadbent, Anthony Brooke, Len Cole, Michael Cole, Peter Collins, R Cooper, Mike Cowling, Peter Dawes, Sandy Doggart, A S Eason, Martyn Flower, Clive Goodwin, Bob Grieves, Douglas Hand, Mr & Mrs Hedges, Mrs Pat Hellier, John Heseltine, J House, Peter Moakes, Sydney Monham, Stewart Mouce, Norman Newbatt, David Newman, Michael O'Hare, A W Payne, Colin J Peck, G A Perrott, Lance R Phillips, Bill Pryor, Ken Purvey, Burt Roberts, Wally Rogers, Keith Scandrett, Mike Seary, Eric Southgate, Frank Spencer, Gerry Stream, Eric Stromberg, Desmond and Raymond Telford, Chris Todd, Guy Tremlett, David Turney, Kenneth Wallace and Ivor Webb.

Finally, I should like to thank all those who raced at Crystal Palace, for without them, and the enjoyment they gave to so many others, there would simply be no story to tell . . .

P.P.

CHAPTER 1

Sir Joseph Paxton's 'greenhouse'

From Hyde Park to Anerley, 1851 to 1911

Some 35 years before the first petrol-engined vehicle had even turned a wheel, in 1849, Albert, the Prince Consort and beloved husband of Queen Victoria, announced his intention to organize a 'Great Exhibition' in London's Hyde Park. No doubt he had been inspired by similar events on the Continent, but he was determined that this would be better than all of them and represent the great British Empire of the Victorian age to its best advantage.

A Royal Commission was appointed to help with the project, its first task being to find a suitable building that could be erected in the park, then dismantled when the exhibition was over, without causing too much damage and disruption to the park, and all at a reasonable cost. After studying some 240 designs, the Commission decided that the most practical one was a vast brick structure, although this was still far from ideal because the cost would be far more than originally budgeted for as a lot of work would be needed to restore Hyde Park once the building had been demolished.

Meanwhile, in Derby, a businessman called Joseph Paxton had designed several glasshouses for the Duke of Devonshire's Chatsworth Estate. Paxton had business interests in railways and general engineering, and he happened to be in London at this time to discuss his railway business with an MP called Ellis. The two men met in the newly constructed Houses of Parliament, and Paxton remarked to Ellis that the acoustics in the Westminster building were very poor and that the proposed building for the Great Exhibition 'looked like being a similar disaster'. Upon hearing this, and other suggestions which Paxton made, Ellis took him to see Lord Granville of the Royal Commission, who was also impressed by what Paxton had to say. The outcome was that Joseph Paxton was given just 10 days to come up with a suitable replacement for the home of the Great Exhibition.

In Derby, Paxton transformed rough sketches into a full working plan and within a week he was back in front of the Royal Commission showing them his most comprehensive design. It was a giant prefabricated greenhouse. Standing 108ft high at its tallest point, 1,848ft long and 408ft in breadth, the vast conservatory was accepted without hesitation by the Royal Commission as the ideal structure for the event. Years ahead of its time, the design meant that the iron girders and glass panels could be made in factories away from London, then transported to Hyde Park for assembly and erection. When the design appeared in *Punch* magazine it was quickly christened 'The Crystal Palace'. . .

By early spring 1851, Paxton's masterpiece was complete and the exhibits for the Great Exhibition were moved into position. They included gold from the prospectors in the Californian Gold Rush, the Colt 45 revolver, Wedgwood pottery, new engineering inventions for the industry of Britain, railways, photography – still in its infancy – and many other commodities and fine arts from all over the Commonwealth and British Empire and beyond. It was a truly magnificent demonstration of Britain's position as the major world power of the age.

On May Day 1851, Queen Victoria officially opened the Great Exhibition in front of an estimated 500,000 people. Before it closed in October that year some 6,000,000 visitors had attended the event, and profits from it, amounting to £186,000, enabled Prince Albert and the Royal Commission to finance the building of the museums in South Kensington.

Joseph Paxton had been knighted for his part in the exhibition, and when the Crystal Palace was dismantled, Sir Joseph, as head of a business consortium, was able to buy back the building for £70,000 and have it transported to Sydenham, in South East London, and erected at Penge Place, a rural estate of some 200 acres, which were landscaped by Edward Milner and George Eyles. In 1854, the Crystal Palace was reopened and soon the Victorians began flocking to the area, now named after the building, to enjoy the facilities offered by the country's first leisure park.

They could stroll up the Grand Centre Walk from the Penge entrance to the Palace, some 2,660ft flanked with London plane trees, marvel at the fountains at the Lower

Basin as the water rose 250ft into the air, lose themselves in the 175ft diameter Tea Maze, walk in the English Landscape Garden or climb the Central Steps to the six sunken gardens like the parterre of an Italian villa, with flower beds, pools and fountains.

The lakes, created as reservoirs for the various water features in the ground, could be used for fishing and boating, and the Intermediate Lake was used for ice skating when sufficiently frozen in winter. An experimental 'pneumatic railway' developed by T W Ramell and utilizing a carriage drawn along a tunnel by air pressure, ran the 600yds between the Sydenham and Penge entrances. Visitors could also arrive at the specially built Low Level station, half-way down Anerley Hill, and take refreshments in the dining room on the first floor. Education was supplied by the world's first School of Practical Engineering, amongst whose pupils was Geoffrey De Havilland, and another part of the park was set aside for the feature Geology and Inhabitants of the Ancient World, with cliffs showing geological strata and the famous Crystal Palace dinosaurs constructed by Waterhouse Hawkins under advice from Professor Richard Owen, who had originally coined the term 'dinosaur'.

On December 31, 1853, completion of this project was marked by a feast held inside the body of the half-built iguanodon. Twenty-six prehistoric monsters stood in the park, as well as various statues, a sphinx and the bust of Sir Joseph Paxton. Several houses were also built in the park, Rock Hills being the home of Paxton himself, and Parklands that of the great cricketer Dr W G Grace, who was often to

The Crystal Palace in all its splendour, having been reconstructed from the earlier building erected in Hyde Park for the Great Exhibition of 1851. Extensive views of the surrounding countryside were provided from the top of the 282ft high towers.

CRYSTAL PALACE. INHABITANTS OF THE ANCIENT WORLD.   57204

Long before motor sports came to Crystal Palace the park hosted many sporting events including boxing, cricket, cycling, skating and soccer, while for those with a taste for ancient times there was a permanent display of no less than 26 prehistoric monsters.

8

Contrasts in architecture. The main Palace building formed a backcloth for a variety of temporary structures erected for the Festival of Empire Exhibition in 1911.

The massive proportions of the Crystal Palace buildings and the full extent of the surrounding grounds could only be adequately appreciated from the air.

be seen playing the game in the park.

Sporting events such as boxing, cricket, cycling, roller skating and soccer, including cup final matches, all found a home at Crystal Palace. Another immensely popular event was the Brock's firework display, which continued long after many other pastimes had ceased. In the Crystal Palace itself, operas and symphony concerts took place regularly as well as organ recitals, festivals, exhibitions and shows of all kinds. On the new site, two towers had been added to the Palace, one at each end: for a penny you could climb to the top of the North Tower and from the 280ft high public gallery you could see Alexandra Palace in North London. In later years, aircraft could be observed as they came into Croydon Airport, the

first home of the infant civil aviation industry. It was even said that on a clear day you could see right to the South Coast.

By the turn of the 20th Century, people were taking 'horseless vehicles' quite seriously, indeed there was even a journal devoted to them, and pioneer motorcyclists in England began to look for a suitable venue to test their machines. Whereas on the Continent, and especially in France, road races were being organized regularly, enthusiasts in England were being hampered by laws which forbade riders to exceed 20mph. Harry and Charlie Collier, two of the very first British motorcycle racers, turned to the cycle tracks on which to test their machines, and London was in the fortunate position of having three suitable venues

– Herne Hill, Canning Town and Crystal Palace. By 1902, the Collier brothers and other pioneers were a familiar sight on the banked Crystal Palace cycle track. Dressed in thick corduroy trousers, leather boots and jackets and wearing cloth caps reversed on their heads, they quickly developed their machines and soon were able to lap the track at 60mph during demonstrations of wild racing. Harry Martin, known as the English Cannonball, was another of these early aces riding his 2¾hp Excelsior.

November 1901 had seen the formation of The Motor Cycling Club, still in existence today and one of the two oldest motor-sporting clubs in Britain. Though best known for its long-distance trials, in which both cars and motorcycles take part, the MCC has also regularly organized speed events, and in April 1902, following a motor exhibition at the Palace, it held its very first race meeting, using both the cycle track and a speed and hill-climbing course which began on a road near the track and finished on the Grand Terrace. There were three classes, for machines catalogued at 1½hp and under, over 1½hp and under 2hp, and over 2hp, and *The Autocar* reported that 'the races were held under NCU rules, pedalling after the start being thereby allowable'. Six events were run, three races and three speed and hill-climbing contests, and the first event, over two heats and a final, was won by T H Tessier on a Werner. Other makes of motorcycle taking part included

Derby, Rex, Chappelle, Excelsior and Blizzard.

But the rapid development of these early machines quickly outgrew the cycle tracks to the point where the racing became potentially very dangerous. By 1907, the soon to be famous TT races had begun in the Isle of Man, and in Surrey, not too far from Crystal Palace, work had begun on the construction of the world's first purpose-made car and motorcycle race circuit, Brooklands, where Hugh Locke-King's dream was to become a reality. Motor sport had found the answer to the problem of where to race cars and bikes legally and in reasonable safety; Brooklands led the way, but within 20 years Crystal Palace would follow.

In the meantime, one of the main events at Crystal Palace during 1911 was the Empire Exhibition, featuring replicas of the Government Buildings of the Commonwealth, which were reproduced in plaster on wooden frames and erected in the park. But even without these major events, Crystal Palace continued to attract huge crowds, especially on Sundays and Bank Holidays, with its variety of sporting entertainments, music, festivals, shows and firework displays, and its attractive gardens with flowers, ponds, fountains, statues and trees. Sir Joseph Paxton's greenhouse had become a vast leisure attraction, and as the Roaring Twenties approached, further developments were in hand which would ensure that the park at Crystal Palace would remain a big draw for the public for many more years to come.

THE CRYSTAL PALACE FOUNDATION & MUSEUM
by Barrie McKay, Chairman, Museum Trust

On a rainswept day in 1979 more than 1,000 people braved the weather to view an exhibition held at the National Recreation Centre on the history of the Crystal Palace. The inspiration behind this came from a number of enthusiastic local residents who had developed something of a passion for the Palace and were keen to attempt partial restoration of the Crystal Palace site.

The exhibition was a success and in response to public interest, not only in the Palace history but also in the site on which the Palace once stood, the exhibition organisers founded the Crystal Palace Foundation. Since then the Foundation, now with over 1,000 members, has devoted thousands of hours to restoring parts of the site and preserving the Victorian remains. As well as providing education and research, and publishing work concerned with the Crystal Palace, the Foundation organises regular talks, film shows and other events reflecting the importance of the Crystal Palace in our history.

In 1981 the Foundation approached the Greater London Council and submitted a practical scheme for a permanent museum on the site as well as for the restoration and reopening of the upper site which had been closed to the public since the Crystal Palace was destroyed by fire in 1936.

The Foundation's recommendations were accepted and work soon began to relandscape Paxton's terraces and

reinstate the original 1854 pathways, stairways and balustrading.

With regard to a museum, the GLC gave the go-ahead for the Foundation to establish this facility within what was the Palace School of Practical Engineering. In addition, the nearby base of Brunel's south water tower was incorporated as part of the museum display.

By 1983 CPF members began adapting the Anerley Hill premises helped by Community Services and other local voluntary organisations.

It was apparent at an early stage that a new roof was needed for the building and that increased funds were required to see the project through. This, together with the planned abolition of the GLC, brought delay and uncertainty. However, just before its demise in 1986, the authority was persuaded to spend £10,000 on a new roof as well as providing a further £21,000 to go towards the installation of heating, lighting and electrics.

With the formation of a Trust to take on the museum responsibility, the way was clear to establish the world's first museum dedicated to the history of the Crystal Palace.

In the meantime, the London Borough of Bromley took over responsibility for the Crystal Palace park and as well as encouraging the museum project and stepping up the restoration of the grounds,

Bromley produced its own masterplan to promote a hotel and leisure structure for the site, designed on the lines of the former Crystal Palace.

In 1988, the former School of Engineering was opened by the Museum Trust as a photographic display of the Crystal Palace. During this time the Museum Trust, with assistance from the Royal Commission for the Exhibition of 1851, arranged for the cataloguing and preparation of the museum collection, and on June 17th 1990 the Duke of Devonshire performed the opening ceremony of the museum.

Visitors to the museum are greeted by a huge mural depicting the interior of the Crystal Palace, with the inside of the museum decorated with greenery, statues and flags of all nations to recreate the atmosphere of the old Palace. In addition to the many historical items on display, including models, porcelain, medals, trophies, books and paintings, the museum features video film of the Palace and music that once could be heard at the Crystal Palace.

**THE CRYSTAL PALACE
FOUNDATION & MUSEUM**
If you are interested in joining the Crystal Palace Foundation or wish to know more about the museum, contact the CPF, 84 Anerley Road, London SE19 2AH. Tel: 081 778 2173.

CHAPTER 2

Motorcycle racing comes to London

Path racing at Crystal Palace Park, 1926 to 1935

In 1926, some motorcycle enthusiasts led by Fred Mockford and Cecil Smith formed a group called London Motor Sports Ltd. Their dream was to see motorcycle road racing on a closed circuit within the capital. By then, racing at Brooklands had become firmly established, and throughout the country various small tracks had emerged, mostly using the unmetalled paths of parks and the grounds of stately homes, on which club riders could race their motorcycles. These included Drayton Manor in Staffordshire (more recently made famous for its amusement park and zoo), Park Hall in Oswestry, Esholt Park in Bradford and a tiny quarry track at Parbold in Lancashire. Syston Park, near Grantham, hosted several meetings before a dispute involving the organizers led to the establishment of a rival venue at Donington Park – but that is another story.

North London would not have its own venue until the 1930s, when a small track was created at Alexandra Palace, but in January 1927 Mockford and Smith, having identified the potential of Crystal Palace Park for racing, put forward a proposal to the Trustees. At first it was received without much enthusiasm, but they persisted with their idea and eventually the Trustees gave their permission for a race meeting to be organized.

A one-mile course was laid out over the paths of the park, and one Sunday morning several riders were invited along to take a test run around the proposed course. They emerged full of enthusiasm, having seen the potential of the scheme, and soon afterwards May 21, 1927 was announced as the date of the inaugural Crystal Palace Road Racing Meeting. It would consist of 10 races, which would be open to members of any motorcycle club within the South-East Centre of the Auto-Cycle Union.

Many of the top riders of the day were on the entry list when it closed on May 2, including W Browning, L Parker, Gordon Norchi and F Pike, who had entered for the rather grandly named sidecar Grand Prix. Entries for the solo Grand Prix included I P Riddoch, Paddy Johnston, T G Meeten, Roy Charman, W A Colgan, Gus Kuhn, G W Limmer and, again, L Parker, all of whom, according to *The Motor Cycle* magazine, 'may be relied upon to demonstrate how a motorcycle should be handled'.

The paths used for the track Mockford and Smith had laid out had been well prepared for racing; all potholes had been filled, a dangerous concrete abutment padded and the bends tarred. The remainder of the track, although still loose-surfaced, was hard-packed and consistent. From the start/finish line on the Centre Walk (between the football and sports grounds) the track led some 200yds to the Maze Hairpin, a 180-degree left-hander, which was followed by a tight right-hander called Three Tree Corner. This in turn led on to a 90-degree right-hand bend called New Zealand Corner (the name being derived from the replica of the New Zealand parliament building which had been erected for the Empire Exhibition in 1911 and still stood nearby). The course then followed a long, sweeping left-hand section to the Statue Hairpin, followed by another left-hander to Rockhills Hairpin and on to a fairly fast and relatively straight section alongside the lake. From there a long, sweeping right-hander skirted round the sports ground and took riders past the timekeeper's box and back across the start/finish line. *The Motor Cycle* magazine predicted that the course would 'provide all the thrills of the TT'. First practising took place on May 9, and several more days were set aside prior to the race to enable competitors to familiarize themselves with the track.

May 21 dawned as a glorious spring morning and the organizers' optimism was rewarded when more than 10,000 Londoners turned up to witness their very own racing circuit in action. To gain admission they each paid a shilling plus two pence in tax (a total of about 6p in modern money) and such was their enthusiasm that many of them ducked under the ropes that had been put up to keep them from straying into the more dangerous areas of the course. The large number of marshals present did their best to keep the crowds in their allocated areas, but the task proved impossible and during one of the races a sidecar combination overshot a bend and ended up amongst the crowd, two of whom were slightly hurt.

At 3pm, after the organizers had fired a maroon to warn the crowd, many of whom were still casually strolling along the track, the first motorized race at Crystal Palace was flagged away. There were only four riders for the Whitehall race for 175cc machines and the crowd were able to identify them by their different coloured pullovers, rather like jockeys' riding silks. They started in pairs at 15-second intervals and Riddoch on his Zenith-Blackburne led the first lap, crossing the line some 300yds ahead of the Francis-Barnett of J D Broughton; the other riders, also on Francis-Barnetts, were J Easter and G C Horsman. Riddoch slowed on lap 2 when his spark plug oiled up and Broughton was able to pass him on lap 3. Then the Zenith began to run a little better, but although he tried hard, Riddoch was unable to catch Broughton, who crossed the finishing line in 12min 8.5sec to write his name in the history books as the first winner of a motorized race at Crystal Palace. Riddoch came home 24sec behind him and Easter finished third.

The second event, the Pall Mall race for 250cc solos, proved to be the most exciting of the day and had the crowd enthralled. Paddy Johnston, riding a Cotton, made the better start of the first pair, although F W Clark and his New Imperial were very close at the Maze Hairpin. The second pair, H C Jefferee and L H Wilson, both riding Dunelts, were engaged in a similar close scrap, and after the first lap the order was Johnston, Clark, Wilson and Jefferee. Then, as the leading pair approached the timekeeper's box on lap 2, Johnston took the bend too fast, ran wide and allowed Clark to take the lead. But not for long because he fell from his machine at New Zealand Bend, and although he remounted, Johnston, who had won the Lightweight TT the previous year, gained a 50yd lead. Clark now began a big charge after Johnston and by lap 5 he had narrowed the gap to some 10yds. As the two riders flashed past the stands for the last time Clark's New Imperial was alongside the Cotton and he took the flag just a fraction of a second ahead, Wilson finishing third, mere yards ahead of Jefferee. The race had thrilled the crowd, who were still cheering long after it was all over.

Most of the races were given 'London' names that day and although some were split into private and trade entry classes, where sufficient entries had been received separate races were run for the two classes. Thus the 350cc Westminster race was for trade riders, attracted 11 entries and was won by F E Parnacott on an AJS, while the private owners' race was won by L Bellamy on a Coventry Eagle, the Kingsway Race for 500cc machines fell to S Twiby on an AJS and the equivalent private owners' race was won by L J Twitchett with a Dunelt.

The main solo event of the day, the Crystal Palace Grand Prix, was over 10 laps, twice the distance of the other events, and Bellamy, one of 15 starters, had a fairly easy win in 22min 8sec, riding his Coventry Eagle. G W Hole, riding a 350cc Raleigh, was second after being challenged in the early stages by Limmer on a 500cc Scott before he took a tumble in front of Hole at Three Tree Corner and lost a lot of time. B Bragg, though, had the most adventurous time before taking third place with his 350cc Coventry Eagle. On lap 2 he fell off at Three Tree Corner, he skidded with

locked brakes past the lake on the next lap, he had another wild skid and stalled on lap 6, nearly hit a tree on lap 7 and narrowly missed the spectators at the Maze Hairpin on lap 9!

Showing commendable patience, the organizers deferred the start of the next race while Limmer completed his last two laps of the previous event all on his own, but in any case, the delayed race, the first of three for sidecars, was less than an epic. There were only three entries, which were started at 15sec intervals, and since two of them dropped out, Parker when his Douglas oiled a plug and Norchi when his Coventry Eagle lost its chain, P R Bradbrook was left to complete the five laps by himself in 11min 45.6sec.

The South Tower race for private owners produced five starters, but although J E Chell was the winner on his AJS, it was the spectacular cornering of A J Dussek and his Norton, who finished second ahead of W Browning's Norton, which mainly entertained the spectators. There was an amusing incident at the end of the first lap when S E Burlington stopped his Norton, peered quizzically down towards his carburettor, then turned to a timekeeper sitting at a nearby table and said 'I think I'll risk it', whereupon the official replied 'Are you using bacon fat as fuel?'.

The 10-lap Crystal Palace Sidecar Grand Prix, which was the final race, produced a superb ride from Norchi, whose Coventry Eagle started 15sec behind Browning's Norton but caught it in three laps, went into the lead on lap 4 when Browning's machine gave trouble and ran out an easy winner in 22min 1sec. L H Dockerill's Coventry Eagle had dropped out after the first lap, so Bradbrook, realising he had no chance of catching the leader unless he ran into problems, decided to take things easy and lit up a cigarette on his way to an undisputed second place! So ended the first motorcycle meeting at Crystal Palace. During the afternoon the fastest lap had been set by Parnacott on his 348cc AJS in 2min 7.4sec, giving Crystal Palace's first lap recordholder an average speed of just 28.2mph!

A few showers had dampened the track towards the end of the day, but they in no way dampened the enthusiasm of competitors, spectators and organizers alike. The riders seemed to think the course was excellent, and the spectators had been thrilled by the racing, which for many of them was the first they had ever seen. They cheered every winner and there was warm applause for the many riders who fell off then gamely remounted and continued with their racing, while the organizers were heartened not only by the size of the turnout of spectators, but also by the enthusiastic response which they and the competitors had given to their idea of bringing motorcycle racing to London. After a speech by Professor Low and the presentation of trophies by Mrs F W Barnes, most people left Crystal Palace that evening very happy with the day's events and eager to return for more.

A few days later the event was discussed in the Talmage column of *The Motor Cycle*, which echoed the crowd's enthusiasm and offered few criticisms. It was suggested that fencing instead of rope might be used to restrain the over-enthusiastic and that the course could be made wider. Also, although the idea of starting bikes at intervals was fine, some sort of scoreboard should be erected to enable spectators to follow the racing more easily. The use of coloured jerseys to help rider identification was praised, but not the suggestion

A map, which was reproduced in the January 20, 1927 issue of *The Motor Cycle* magazine, revealed how some of the pathways in the Crystal Palace grounds below the Terrace were converted into a race circuit for the first motorcycle meetings, and temporary pits and a paddock area were provided between the football and sports grounds.

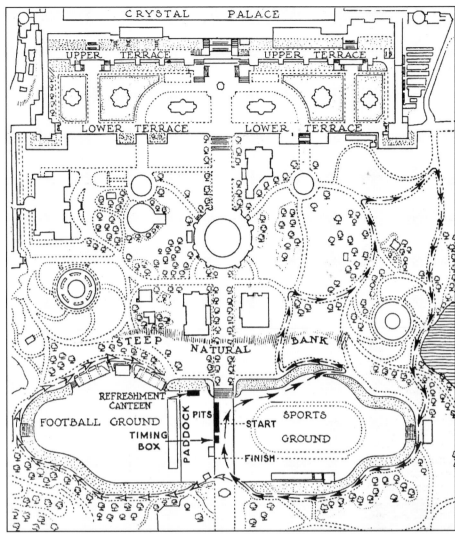

F E Parnacott on a 350cc Raleigh leading Taiby's AJS through the Maze Hairpin during a preliminary heat of the Newmarket Cup race in 1927, the first season of path racing at Crystal Palace. During the inaugural meeting on May 21, Parnacott, who rode a 350cc AJS on that occasion, had been credited with the first official lap record at just over 28mph!

13

The sidecar events often provided the high points of early Crystal Palace race meetings, the athletic prowess of passengers regularly being put to the test on the bumpier sections of the paths. Here L J Pellatt's 346cc OK Supreme leads G A Norchi's 346cc Coventry Eagle at Three Tree Corner.

that the corners should be banked and the entire track surface made hard, which was felt to be unnecessary. Some of the trees should be trimmed or removed (one competitor had ridden straight through a holly bush, leaving a tunnel through it before carrying on racing!) and some of the low branches should be cut away as several sidecar passengers had almost been beheaded at one point. Finally, it was suggested that several dangerous concrete projections should be either padded or removed.

Some concern was also voiced in higher places. A month after the inaugural meeting, the question of the two injured spectators was raised in the House of Commons when Colonel Day asked the Home Secretary if he was aware of the incident and what instructions had been issued to ensure that something similar could not happen again. Sir W Joynson-Hicks replied that he had made an inquiry and was not satisfied with the safety precautions at Crystal Palace that day. He explained that the Police had not been consulted about the event, but had since made suggestions to the organizers which should ensure that nothing of a similar nature would occur again.

Meanwhile, Mockford and Smith, in preparation for a second race meeting, were already making several improvements to the course, including widening much of it, removing some lamp standards near the timekeeper's box, and tarring much of the loose sections from the Maze Hairpin to the Statue Hairpin and from the Rockhills

Hairpin down past the lake and stand stretches. A dangerous adverse camber with a loose surface near the lake was raised by a foot and resurfaced, and at the bottom of this descent a potentially very dangerous concrete and steel abutment was removed. They also invested some £500 installing a permanent crash barrier around nearly all of the track, some 15ft from the edge of the roadway. In addition, a loudspeaker system was installed for the benefit of the crowd.

The wider track meant that the organizers could adopt a new format for the races. In future, competitors would be divided into groups of four and be lined up four abreast on the start line for a series of two-lap heats, the winner of each of which would go forward to a five-lap final. A maximum of 16 riders would be allowed on the course at one time, enabling four heats to be run simultaneously. In the event of more than 16 riders being entered for a race, two batches of heats would be run, to be followed by semi-finals for the heat winners, from which the four finalists would emerge. To help spectators with identification, all riders in a heat would be required to wear the same coloured jersey, a different colour being chosen for each heat. This meant that the four finalists would each be wearing a different coloured jersey. It was anticipated that the changes would result in higher speeds, more competitive racing and, as a result of more riders on the track, greater interest for the spectators, who would also be better protected. Finally, as a nice touch for the competitors, Mockford and Smith decided to employ an engraver at the track, who would inscribe the relevant trophies as soon as the race results were known.

Entrants for the second meeting, to be staged on August 6, were charged 5 shillings (25p) for the 175cc, 250cc, 350cc and 500cc solo and 600cc and unlimited sidecar events, and a guinea (£1.05) for the Crystal Palace Solo Championship, the winner of which would receive a handsome trophy donated by *The Motor Cycle*. By the time entries closed on July 18, Cecil Smith had the names of 126 competitors for the programme. Practice sessions were held on the evenings of July 26 and 27 and during the afternoon of July 30 in addition to the hour-long session on race morning.

With an attendance of some 16,000 people the meeting was another triumph for Mockford and Smith, and this time the spectators were much better behaved, standing obediently behind the barriers, where they were kept well

informed of the progress of races through the new loudspeakers. *The Motor Cycle*, commenting on the meeting afterwards, wrote that 'racing has come to stay at Crystal Palace and the sport bids fair to outrival cricket, football or even greyhound racing; the Crystal Palace is easy of access, the price of admission is within easy reach of everyone's means, and the racing is so crammed with excitement and good sportsmanship that it has to be seen to be realised'.

The individual races were named after horse racing venues, and the Wye Cup for 175cc machines was won by Broughton, whose Francis-Barnett, equipped – unusually for the time – with a front-wheel brake, gained the lead on the first lap and remained in front to the end. The Epsom Cup for sidecars brought a win for Norchi's Coventry Eagle, with F H Brackpool's Matchless not far behind, but Gus Kuhn stole most of the attention when his passenger almost lost his

Fred Brackpool, one of the Crystal Palace stalwarts and amongst its most prominent riders during the early years, tackling Three Tree Corner on his highly tuned 347cc Matchless combination.

Harold Daniell, who was to have a brilliant career ahead of him as a Norton road-racer, leads the field through the Maze Hairpin during the murk of a November day in 1928 with the Velocettes of Gilbert, Wood and Hewstone in pursuit.

trousers after the buttons on his braces failed to stand the pace; the last one came loose as Kuhn started his final lap!

Broughton went on win the 250cc Ascot Cup after a race-long scrap with J W Troughton.

The main race of the day was full of incidents. The brakes failed on W W Fuller's Coventry Eagle as he descended the slope past the lake, and as his machine entered the water Fuller flew through the air and landed in the lake some distance from the bank and had to swim ashore. Gus Kuhn led the final, but came into the pits after two laps believing the race to be over. A F H Tunbridge then took the lead only to be black-flagged off the course when the exhaust pipe of his Calthorpe started to come adrift. This enabled P F Parker to take over the lead with his Cotton until he, too, suffered a loose exhaust and was subsequently disqualified, although he had led across the finishing line. The trophy, therefore, went to Bellamy, riding a Coventry Eagle, although Kuhn had the satisfaction of setting the fastest lap in 1min 56sec, and he went on to win the Kempton Cup race on his 350cc Velocette, despite the fact that his cigarette went out on lap 4; he resisted the urge to relight it until after the race!

The Catterick Cup for sidecars was the best race of the day with a hard-fought duel between Norton riders Dussek and L T Truett, closely followed by a bunch consisting of C F Stokes and Chell on AJSs and G Templeman on another Norton. The fiercest battle of all was between Chell and Stokes, but it ended when Stokes, who had been passed on the inside at the Maze Hairpin on lap 3, attempted to repass Chell on the narrow Stand Stretch and the two combinations collided, one of them being somersaulted down the steep grass bank. There were further wins for Norchi and his Coventry Eagle and K Pugh on a 350cc OK Supreme in the Newmarket Cup, but by then dusk was approaching and four more races had to be deferred to the next meeting.

It took place on September 17, and this time the crowd had grown to 17,000, despite the wet conditions during the morning when, due to the extra races to be accommodated in the programme, it was decided to run some of the preliminary heats. Fortunately the weather improved for the main part of the meeting. Gus Kuhn had an easy win in the opening Newmarket Cup race on his Velocette, then the crowd were thrilled to see three 1,000cc twins lining up for the first sidecar race; it was the first time anything larger than a 600cc machine had been seen at the Palace. But their expected power advantage did little for them in the race and the only one of the trio to finish, the Matchless of A E Webb, was beaten into second place by Truett's 500cc Norton. Of the others, M A Angell's McEvoy stopped on the circuit and had to be pushed across the finishing line, while C W Sewell's Brough Superior shed its chain going past the timekeeper's box, the commentator being greeted with howls of laughter when he announced the reason for retirement as tyre trouble at the very moment a marshal was retrieving the broken chain from the track. Though Norchi looked to be unbeatable in the trade section of this race, a troublesome sidecar wheel meant that he had to get off and push for part of his last lap, which allowed C Pallanza to take the chequered flag with his Triumph.

The big event of the 12-race meeting was the Autumn Cup for 500cc machines. The first heat was won by Parnacott on a Raleigh, despite nearly hitting another rider who had fallen off at the Maze Hairpin, the second heat gave Kuhn another comfortable win and the third was won by A Foulds on a Sunbeam, but it was Heat 7 which provided the thrills as A H Willimott on his HRD and W G Chable on a Norton diced for the honours. Chable tried to outbrake the HRD as they approached the final curve, just made it, but then hit a large bump and flew into the air, landing just in front of Willimott. Somehow he managed to stay on his Norton and crossed the line just inches ahead of the HRD. The final was also a thriller, with Gus Kuhn leading all the way but being gradually hauled in by A Foulds' Sunbeam. The gap behind Kuhn's Velocette became smaller every lap, but when within striking distance on the final lap Foulds made a slight mistake beside the lake and took a tumble, rolling down the grass bank, fortunately without injury. Chable continued to entertain the crowd at the Maze Hairpin, almost falling off on the first two laps and finally doing so after hitting the bank on lap 3.

The Leicester Cup for 250cc machines featured bikes with such unlikely names as The Gasoline Hare and The Paraffin Hound, but they could not match the pace of 'Nobby' Clark's Coventry Eagle. P F Parker crashed his Francis-Barnett very heavily and lay still beside it, telling the St John Ambulance men he was unable to move. The doctor was called, but after giving Parker a thorough examination he instructed the rider to 'take up thy machine and walk' because he could find nothing wrong with him!

The Doncaster Cup for sidecars saw Twitchett, who had ridden The Gasoline Hare in the previous race, acting as passenger for Bellamy's Coventry Eagle, christened Ma Wee Haggis, but they proved no match for winner Norchi. Gus Kuhn scored yet another win in the Goodwood Cup race and there were sidecar wins for R V Newman (Matchless) and J G Richards (Scott), but Norchi once again had trouble with his sidecar's wheel when the lug attaching it to the chassis broke, and the final race of the day went to Willimott on his HRD.

At the prizegiving the popular Gus Kuhn had to enlist the help of two small girls to help him carry off all his trophies, while Norchi solved the problem of how to ride his broken outfit home by fitting a skid plate in place of his missing sidecar wheel. So ended the first season of racing at the Palace in a mood of mutual congratulations. All three meetings had been highly successful ventures, and public interest had grown steadily, which encouraged Mockford and Smith to press ahead with their plans for 1928. The formula was to be largely as before, but they decided to scrap the individual sections for trade and private riders and instead to group the riders into A and B grades according to their experience and ability.

Riders were back at the track on March 11 for a practice session for the first 1928 meeting to be held the following weekend, and most of the regulars were there, many of them with new or modified machines. Gus Kuhn turned up with two Calthorpes, Brackpool had two specially built Matchless outfits, there were several short-wheelbase Bakers and a 172cc P and P, featuring an open frame and a saddle height barely 15in from the ground. Several Brooklands riders had entered to give Crystal Palace a try, including W H Phillips,

Tommy Hall holding a narrow lead over Fred Neill in an Essex Cup race. Note the Brooklands-type fishtail silencer fitted to Hall's machine.

who had a streamlined JAP-engined Cotton.

Once again race day was blessed with fine weather and 19,000 people turned up to watch five events, each consisting of two races, one for A-grade and one for B-grade riders, and it was to prove a day full of incidents. In the B-grade race for 350cc sidecars Clark hit a press photographer who had wandered too close to the track, then in the A-grade 600cc sidecar race Norchi and Brackpool were enjoying a huge scrap when the plug oiled on Norchi's Coventry Eagle. Norchi stopped to have the plug cleaned, leaving Brackpool to be chased by Driscoll's Norton, but as Driscoll tore past the stand the forks of his outfit broke, launching both rider and passenger down the bank, Driscoll receiving a bang on the head which left him unconscious for a while. Meanwhile, Norchi had rejoined the race, but was unable to do anything about Brackpool, although he did take 2 seconds off the Matchless rider's lap record, leaving it at 2min 3sec. There was another spectacular incident in the second heat when A Noterman managed to do a complete somersault and then roll down the bank near the Stand Stretch when he lost control of his Triumph.

Although Gus Kuhn had managed to win his heat on his new Calthorpe, he was unable to beat C S Barrow's Royal Enfield in the final of the Maidstone Cup for 350cc solos, and similarly in the 500cc race he was being led by the Sunbeam of Palace newcomer H G Lewis when the chain of his Calthorpe broke. The meeting ended with a victory for

F G Hicks, whose 350cc Velocette combination defeated Brackpool's Matchless, Pellat's OK Supreme and Norchi's Coventry Eagle.

A date clash with a meeting at Brooklands and a thunderstorm and downpour on race morning meant that the crowd was slightly down for the next meeting on April 11, and a further disappointment was that Norchi, by now an established Palace favourite, was unwell and failed to feature in any of his races. A special three-lap match race was added to the programme featuring Gus Kuhn and his arch-rival Barrow. Kuhn won the toss and took the inside starting position, from which he made the better start, Barrow's Royal Enfield following him about a yard behind. Then, on lap 2, Barrow made a rare mistake at Three Tree Corner and broke a footrest, and Kuhn, unaware of his rival's problem, continued at unabated pace until he crossed the line to the cheers of the crowd.

Many of the races that day turned out to be as dull as the weather, but there were a few incidents to lift the interest. Hole managed to catch the padding protecting one of the concrete walls with his Raleigh sidecar outfit, which on the next lap appeared with his passenger endeavouring to remove straw from the machine's wheels, while Kuhn had problems on the slippery track during the 500cc race, falling off at the Maze Hairpin and remounting, only to climb the bank just a few yards further on. Brackpool, however, did remarkably well in pulverising the unlimited A-grade sidecar lap record with his 500cc Matchless despite the wet and slippery track.

Another form of motorcycle sport, speedway, or dirt-track racing as it was originally known, had just arrived in Britain from Australia and was beginning to draw huge crowds. Mockford and Smith were watching this development with great interest, but they decided to continue to concentrate on promoting path racing, at least for the time being, and at the end of May they staged their third meeting of the year, this time in beautiful sunshine, which attracted out the usual large crowd. Many of the regular competitors added trophies to their shelves that day, there being wins for Bellamy (Coventry Eagle), Hole (Raleigh), L Lancaster (Cotton), Clark (New Imperial) and two for Brackpool and his Matchless outfit. A young man by the name of Kenneth Dixon on an OK Supreme impressed many people that day when he beat the established stars, including Kuhn and Hole, in the 350cc solo race, while Fay Taylour demonstrated that it was not only men who could ride motorcycles when she did a couple of exhibition laps on her 350cc Rudge Whitworth. While she was unable to repeat her best practice time of 2min 1.2sec (due, she said, to 'stage fright'), she turned in the quite respectable times of 2min 9sec, then 2min 6.2sec, which were faster than many of the male competitors could manage that day.

Although by this time dirt-track racing was proving a huge draw all over the country, including Crystal Palace, a good crowd was still prepared to brave the heavy showers on July 1 for the next path racing meeting, many of them attracted by the prospect of witnessing the special match race between Fay Taylour and another lady rider, Betty Petherwick, on an Ariel. Although Taylour followed the Ariel for most of the two-lap race she sped past in the closing stages, her Rudge Whitworth crossing the line the winner by a handsome margin. During one of the sidecar races Brackpool lowered the lap record to 1min 58.2sec, while in the Sidecar Grand Prix Norchi amused the crowd by losing his passenger at the Maze hairpin. He stopped

while the unfortunate man sprinted back to the machine and completed the race, after which the passenger remarked ruefully 'about 20,000 people must have seen me vacate the sidecar', whereupon the reporter from *The Motor Cycle* assured him that 'about 160,000 people will read about it next Thursday'! Brackpool took another fifth of a second off the lap record on his way to victory, leaving it just 4 seconds slower than Gus Kuhn's solo record. Newman (Matchless) and Sewell (Brough Superior) entertained the crowd with their spirited dice for second place, which Newman won, Sewell having to be consoled by the ovation he received from the crowd for his efforts. The afternoon's racing was completed by a match race between Kuhn and Hole, the former's Calthorpe taking the honours.

By the time of the August meeting many of the regular competitors had been tempted away from path racing to the dirt-track, Kuhn, Norchi, Bellamy, Brackpool and Lewis being amongst those missing. This time, the Crystal Palace Motor Cycle Racing Club, under the auspices of Mockford and Smith, had been able to attract only a disappointingly small crowd, despite the cloudless skies and sub-tropical heat. All but one of the races were named after counties, and the 175cc Kent Cup went to A Sharp on a Zenith, Clark took the Surrey Cup for 250cc bikes with his New Imperial, E Turner the Essex Cup for 500cc machines on his Velocette, and Lancaster's 350cc Velocette took him to victory in the Middlesex Cup race. The main event of the day, the Crystal Palace Solo Grand Prix, was won by F W Neill on a 500cc Matchless, but the crowd were as much amused by the voice of his chief supporter as by his own riding skill. This man, rumoured to be a sergeant-major, roared 'Come on Fred!' so mightily from the grandstand that his shouts even drowned the noise of the bikes!

Two more fixtures completed the 1928 season, *The Motor Cycle* Cup meeting on November 3 and the Crystal Palace Sidecar Championship on November 29, both meetings taking place in cold but dry weather. The entry list for the latter event included Roger Frogley, who had

J W Forbes on his 172cc Baker Villiers leading a trio of solos through Three Tree Corner during the opening meeting of the 1929 season, held on a bitterly cold afternoon in March.

made quite a name for himself in speedway racing, but he seemed unable to adapt to the path circuit. After falling off his Scott three times in one race and even taking a tumble in the paddock he decided to limit his involvement to presenting the prizes in order to avoid further embarrassment! Clark was the recipient of the Penge Cup and the Blackheath Cup went to Harold Daniell on his Norton after a titanic struggle with Kuhn's Calthorpe, which finished second, and R R Barber's Matchless.

A special match race with a £5 wager for the Norwood Cottage Hospital featuring R S Inglis on a 172cc Baker and H Lester on a 172cc SOS rather fell apart when a disgruntled Lester had to push his bike across the line after it had broken down on the first lap, while the main event, the Sidecar Championship, was spoiled by the large number of retirements, Newman and Brackpool emerging first and second on their 500cc Matchless machines. In the final event, the A-grade race went to Bellamy on his Coventry Eagle and the B-grade Catford Cup race, which was held in semi-darkness, to H M Lawrence and his Velocette.

Despite the increasing popularity of speedway racing, there was still sufficient support for path racing to persuade Mockford and Smith to prepare a 1929 programme, which began on March 16 in bitterly cold weather. The racing was to prove rather unexciting that day, and one spectator was particularly disappointed that no-one had taken a plunge into the lake; he had travelled down from New Barnet having been assured that a trip into the water was a regular occurrence at the Palace! Most races lacked any drama, but when Brackpool retired with a misfire from the sidecar race after challenging for the lead he immediately protested to the ACU steward that someone had put sawdust in his petrol tank, producing a carburettor with sawdust attached as evidence! Newman was the victor of both sidecar races and Daniell took the 500cc solo event.

An evening meeting was staged by London Motor Sports on June 19 in front of a large crowd. The corners had received a new coating of tar, but the combination of the hot sun on them and the cornering of the sidecars soon tore it up, making the track very treacherous, especially for the solo riders. *The Motor Cycle* reported 'a clubbish atmosphere in the paddock and – all too rare in these days of stripped racing machinery – several of the competitors were using fully equipped road machines', which suggests that the professionals were taking over sooner than one might have thought!

The entries included Triss Sharp, who was much better known on the speedway track, as became clear by the way he broadsided in dirt-track style at the Maze Hairpin on his way to victory in the 250cc race with his Zenith. Sharp was narrowly beaten in the 350cc event by R R Barner's Matchless, T F Hall took the 500cc race and H Preston the novice race. Brackpool took one sidecar qualifier and H R Taylor the other, but the Grand Prix provided a win for Newman's Matchless after a race enlivened by R Astell's successful attempt to wrap his Triumph round one of the lamp standards.

The evening meeting had been sufficiently successful for another to be run in July, when once again the track, baked by the summer sun, was quite loose and treacherous, resulting in some spectacular cornering. The delightful informality of these evening events was typified by the decision to delay the start of the first race while one of the riders, S Deller, went in search of his 'lost' machine; he eventually found the 172cc Baker in the back of his car, then used it to win the race! As usual the sidecars provided good entertainment and produced another win for Brackpool, and the Grand Prix for solos developed into an exciting scrap between Daniell and Hall, the latter's Matchless winning after Daniell's machine had hit trouble. As a novelty, a lighthearted interlude race was staged between the ACU steward A G Pickering and the judge of the meeting, F Pike, both of them driving Austin Sevens with passengers aboard to help with the cornering. The first ever car race at Crystal Palace went to Mr Pike, who covered the two laps at an average speed of just 22.08mph!

The Crystal Palace Solo Championship for *The Motor Cycle* Trophy was also staged as an evening event, in August, but unfortunately the weather on this occasion was dull with the threat of rain, which kept most of the usual crowd away. Also missing was the current holder of the trophy, Bellamy, whose absence left Daniell to dominate the race on his Norton, with which he twice broke Gus Kuhn's long-standing lap record on his way to victory. First he lowered it by two-fifths of a second from a standing start, then he lapped the track in 1min 50.6sec to set the new record at an average of 33mph, giving the few spectators present memories of a fine display of machine control. Another to impress and break a lap record was Fred Brackpool on his way to his customary sidecar win after a thrilling battle, while Triss Sharp had some dramatic moments during the 175cc race. Struggling with a loose petrol pipe on his Zenith, he missed his braking point for the Maze Hairpin and rather than hit the spectators he laid the bike down, repaired the broken union, restarted and set off once more. However, in stopping his bike he must have banged his head, for a few yards on he blacked out and crashed heavily, being lucky to be able to walk back to the paddock bruised and shaken but otherwise unhurt. Inspired by the novelty race at the previous meeting, a race for baby cars completed the programme and attracted four Austins, a Singer and an MG Midget. The cars, it was said, lacked 'the noise, acceleration and braking' of their two-wheeled counterparts, and how five cars managed to overtake each other on a track that was only 12ft wide at most parts remains a mystery!

The track was in very poor condition after rain had made many parts of it sticky and the remainder of the surface had become very loose when the final event of the year was held on November 9. Lester took the honours in the 175cc race with his SOS and Daniell won the 500cc race from Brooklands regular Tommy Hall on a Matchless. Brackpool seemed to be on his way to his usual sidecar win when he made a rare mistake and overturned his Matchless combination. He and his passenger quickly righted and restarted the machine, took off after the pack and actually regained the lead, but the crash had loosened the sidecar wheel and Brackpool lost control, rolling the outfit over once again and allowing Truett's Norton through to win.

A special match race between Daniell and Hall then thrilled the crowd. Hall, more used to racing on the smoother surface at Brooklands, struggled to keep his Matchless ahead of Daniell, controlling his bucking and snaking machine with great skill. Try as he did, Daniell could not pass the Matchless, which was powered by a special Brooklands engine capable of taking it to a top speed of over 100mph. Though hampered by inferior acceleration and having his spectacles broken by a stone, Daniell made a supreme effort on the last lap, but he tried just a little too hard and lost control of his Norton on the Stand Stretch. Hall crossed the line while Daniell picked himself up, restarted the bike and toured back to the paddock, highly amused by his tumble. After the race, the modest Hall said he really did not know how he had managed to keep Daniell behind and that he had needed every ounce of power from his bike. He went on to say that an hour of racing at Brooklands was less exhausting than three laps of Crystal Palace!

By 1930 Mockford and Smith were devoting much of their time to speedway racing at the Palace, and by the summer, no meetings having been run on the path racing track that year, letters were being printed in the motorcycle press asking what had become of the racing there, and many people, spectators and competitors alike, were bemoaning its absence. Members of the Crystal Palace Motor Cycle Racing Club were becoming increasingly inquisitive, asking such questions as: 'Could not some other club organize a meeting? Could another park in the south-east provide an alternative venue? Where was the 500 Guinea Trophy the Trustees of the Park had put up for a path racing event? Had it been used for a speedway competition instead? Did Mockford and Smith find the dirt track more profitable? Why had the organizers not provided a balance sheet?'

The grounds of Alexandra Palace and the roadways around Wembley Stadium were suggested as alternatives, but the Sydenham MCC found a site five miles from Crystal Palace where they staged a grass track meeting on a course which included a downhill S-bend, a quarter-mile straight and a 1 in 4 ascent. It attracted many of the Palace regulars, including Daniell, Brackpool, Sewell, Hayward and Cornwell, and was such a success that it was decided on the spot to run a further event.

Meanwhile, H D Roberts, the treasurer of the Streatham and District MCC, had approached Mockford and Smith with the proposal that his club should organize an event at the Palace, the takings to be shared on a 50:50 basis. Roberts was told that there was no chance of any other club being able to promote such a meeting as Mockford and Smith were planning to organize one for the early autumn of 1930. When the event failed to materialize Roberts wrote to *The Motor Cycle*, suggesting to enthusiasts that 'as long as the Crystal Palace dirt track is open there will be no path racing meetings'. But finally, in October 1933, four years after the previous race meeting had been held there, the Streatham club gained the reward for their persistence when they were able to announce that 68 competitors, including many 'old faces' such as Norchi, Daniell, Clark, Kuhn and Phillips, had entered for a Crystal Palace revival meeting to be run on October 28. Practice would take place on the previous Saturday and adult spectators would be charged 1s 3d (about 6p) for admission on race day and children 7d (less than 3p).

But the weather was miserable that day, beginning very cold and dull and ending with a downpour, and only 5,400 turned up to watch. At 2.30pm racing star Jimmy Simpson officially reopened the track with a lap of honour on his Norton, complete with a sports sidecar, and this was followed by a parade of competitors aboard their racing machines, which ranged from TT Replicas to 'Palace Specials' and even included some mud-splattered trials machines which, in view of the state of the track, seemed not to be all that out of place. After the warning maroon had been fired, the first race, for the G M Cook Cup, got under way and provided the only close dice of the meeting, D J Moloney (Velocette), F Harvey (Vincent HRD) and S H Goddard (Excelsior) scrapping throughout and, after a near-disaster at the final bend, crossing the line almost as one, Harvey just getting the decision from Moloney. Daniell was first in his heat then went on to easily win the final after fighting off a challenge from Hall's Rudge.

Spectators warmed themselves by running from corner to corner during the Godfrey Sidecar Cup race to witness the entertaining acrobatics of the passengers, Taylor emerging the race winner with his Norton. Norchi had the misfortune of seeing the passenger of his AJS knock himself out on the hand rail of his sidecar, while Jack Surtees suffered an oiled-up spark plug and W F Friend took a spectacular tumble when his Scott crashed at the Maze Hairpin. The Solo Championship race was divided into eight heats and a final and darkness was falling as Daniell took another win from J C Gilbert and Jock West on Velocette and Ariel, respectively. Chapman and Surtees were allowed to have a private race to close the programme after each of them had had problems during their sidecar heats, and as the crowd began to leave in the pouring rain the growing darkness was lit by the red hot glow from the exhaust pipe of Surtees' Excelsior. It had been a successful comeback for the Crystal Palace track, despite the bad weather.

Pleased with their efforts, the Streatham club named April 7, 1934 as the date of their next meeting on the path circuit and they put together an ambitious programme of 30 heats, semi-finals and finals. Despite a 3pm start, it was gone 7pm on a cold, foggy evening before the final race was to finish. Once again Harold Daniell was the star of the meeting, enjoying two exciting races with Gilbert and his Velocette. Daniell's Norton won the 350cc solo final quite easily, but a fall in the 500cc race meant that Gilbert almost beat him to the line. The sidecars were started singly to avoid any incidents at the first corner, but an interesting duel quickly developed between Sewell (Norton), Surtees (JAP) and Horton (Norton), Sewell gaining the decision in both their races. During one of them, Harold Taylor's Norton provided a thrill for the crowd when it narrowly missed a lamp-post and disappeared into the bushes in a spectacular somersault, fortunately without injury to rider or passenger.

A further 30 races filled the programme of the Streatham club's next meeting, held on May 12, a warm and dry day which helped to bring out a large crowd. They were treated to the sight of a novel form of mass start in which competitors sprinted to their machines, Le Mans-style, from the opposite side of the track and then had to start them up and race away. Gilbert won both the sprint and the race in the 350cc final, scoring an easy win over E J Knox's

CRYSTAL PALACE'S FIRST SEASON

The report in *The Motor Cycle* magazine of the August 1927 meeting spoke of a crowd of 15,000 spectators, and quite a few of them were congregated here as Fred Brackpool and his passenger went by on their 495cc Matchless.

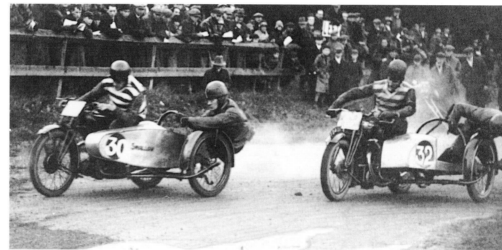

L J Pellatt eases his 344cc OK Supreme ahead of G W Hole's 498cc Raleigh at the Maze Hairpin during the November 1928 meeting.

An unconventional way to take a corner. A Clasan and his passenger arrive at the apex several feet ahead of their Raleigh combination.

Norton. J B Hyde and W G Dark managed to lock the handlebars of their Rudges as they crossed the line and were launched into the air, fortunately without injury, while H J Addie (Velocette) and G Pherenz (Norton) both scored wins in the consolation races. The two sidecar events attracted only four riders, Horton winning one of them and Sewell the other, both on Nortons.

The club held a fourth meeting on July 2, but following a long spell of hot weather the track had become very dusty and loose and was in a generally poor condition. Several races were run on a handicap basis for the first time and a relay race, which was won by a team from the Sydenham MCC, enlivened the afternoon. Gilbert took the final of the 350cc race, but he had to be content with second place in

the 500cc event after his Velocette was beaten by V A Bryant's similar machine, and he could only manage another second behind the AJS of F B Trenholme in the unlimited final. Taylor (Norton) and E Ducker (AJS) were the winners of the two sidecar races.

That evening the crowd went home unaware that they had just witnessed the final path race meeting to be held at Crystal Palace. Speedway, too, had declined in popularity by this time, and in September 1935 rumours about a London Grand Prix to be staged on a real road racing circuit began to appear in the specialist press. A chapter in Crystal Palace's motor sporting history had drawn to a close, but another even more exciting one was shortly to begin, preceded by a disastrous fire which would destroy the Palace itself.

Gus Kuhn and C S Barrow staged a special match race during the April 1928 meeting. Here Kuhn and his 348cc Calthorpe hold a narrow lead over Barrow's 344cc Royal Enfield.

At the previous meeting, a month earlier, R S Deller also had to work hard on his 172cc Baker to resist the challenge of W S Mayhew's 172cc Francis Barnett.

CHAPTER 3

Cinders, speedway and The Glaziers

Racing on a quarter-mile oval, 1928 to 1939

Four years before path racing had even begun at Crystal Palace, on the other side of the world a young New Zealander was living in New South Wales, Australia, working as a secretary to the Hunter Valley Agricultural Society. John S Hoskins had been born in 1892 and had led an adventurous life full of diverse activities prior to arriving in New South Wales. Ever the entrepreneur, he suggested to the Society that they might like to include motorcycle racing on the programme for their annual Electric Light Carnival, which was next due to be held in West Maitland on December 15, 1923. Somewhat reluctantly they agreed, hoping that it might help to boost the falling attendance figures for the event.

Johnny Hoskins quickly laid out an oval dirt track and contacted many of his fellow motorcycle enthusiasts to ensure that the race was well supported. On carnival day, mid-summer in Australia, a large crowd arrived to watch the bikes lap the oval track. Soon they were enthralled by the sight of the riders as they spectacularly broadsided their machines, one foot down through the corners, and despite the showers of cinders thrown up into their faces they loved every minute of it!

Soon the racing had spread through Australia as speedway meetings were held at many new venues, always attracting a large and enthusiastic crowd. Towards the end of 1926, a young Cambridge undergraduate, Lionel Wills of the W D & H O Wills tobacco family, was amongst the crowd at the Sydney Royale meeting. A keen motorcyclist, he too was captivated by the racing and after the meeting he tracked down Johnny Hoskins to find out more about it. He wrote home to England full of enthusiasm for the new sport, which soon he was trying for himself.

When he returned home for Christmas 1927 he was determined that speedway racing should travel with him. He approached Fred Mockford and Cecil Smith, who expressed interest, and the three of them obtained permission from Sir Henry Buckland and the Trustees of the Palace Park to go ahead with the construction of a speedway track at Crystal Palace to be used to supplement the successful path races.

The football ground next to the sports field offered the ideal site for speedway since it already had grandstands which had been erected for the Football Association Cup Finals played there before the First World War. Furthermore, located beneath the seating areas were showers and changing rooms, which had been provided for the soccer players but would prove just as useful for removing the cinders and grime from speedway riders.

A small hut was available for the use of the timekeeper, referee and commentator, and for those who could not afford the price of a grandstand seat most of the football pitch was surrounded by a large earth bank, affording an excellent view over virtually the entire track.

Richard Crittall Ltd were contracted to lay out a 440yd cinder track around the football pitch (which was home to the Corinthian amateur team) and the stands were refurbished and repainted. Finally, when a double-sprung mesh safety fence had been erected around the entire oval at a cost of some £5,000, Crystal Palace was ready to welcome speedway racing.

While all this activity was going on in South London, the new sport had already made the journey from the Antipodes. After a couple of false starts, the first successful British speedway meeting was held at the site of an old athletics track at King's Oak, Epping Forest, in Essex. Surrounded by tall trees, the track soon became known as High Beech. Mr R J Hill-Bailey and the Ilford Motor Cycle Club had laid out a large oval and organized the first speedway meeting there on February 19, 1928.

Some Australian experts were on hand to give advice to the British novices, and the organizers predicted that about 3,000 people would turn up for the 11am start. But when the roads leading to the venue became choked with traffic and every available ticket had been sold within a few minutes of the opening they realized that speedway was bigger than they had bargained for. In the end, some 30,000 people arrived, and they lined both sides of the track, with many more climbing trees to get a view. The organizers were very concerned for spectators' safety because there was no barrier around the track, but fortunately there were no serious incidents.

Fred Ralph claimed the honour of scoring the first win at a speedway meeting in England, and other winners that day included Ivor Creek, Eric Spencer and Colin Watson. The Australian riders received a huge cheer from the crowd as they broadsided their machines spectacularly, Keith Mackay, Billy Galloway, Hilary Buchanan and Stewart St George all thrilling the spectators with their expertise. The day was an unbelievable success. For the organizers it proved just what a draw speedway racing could be; for the riders it demonstrated that to be a winner you had to ride like the Australians; and for the crowd the thrills of this new sport generated an enthusiasm which was to grow continuously over the next few years. The next day the *Daily Mirror* carried the story of the meeting as its main headline, news of speedway quickly spread throughout the UK and within a year 70 new tracks had been constructed.

All this enthusiasm could not have escaped the notice of Mockford and Smith as they oversaw the finishing touches of their track, and posters all over London announced their first meeting, to be held on May 19, 1928. The day was very wet, but this did not deter 20,000 people from arriving at the Palace that afternoon to pay a shilling (5p) admission fee or sixpence (2½p) for children and witness London's first sight of the sport that was sweeping the nation. The ground was soon packed to capacity, but the incessant rain had caused the loudspeaker system to fail, so the announcements were being made by megaphone by the time the first race began, half an hour behind schedule because of the appalling weather.

This heat featured the Australian expert Ron Johnston (345cc Harley-Davidson) and Lionel Wills (500cc Rudge Whitworth), who had the more powerful machine and was able to match Johnston on the straights, but Johnston's skill at broadsiding through the curves gave him a slight advantage. However, his engine hesitated on lap 3 and Wills shot through to win the race, much to the delight of the spectators.

Heat 2 saw the England v Australia fortunes reversed when Sig Schlam (Harley-Davidson) and Les Blakeborough diced for the honours. After two laps Blakeborough's Cotton expired and Schlam carried on in a spectacular manner before his engine also died on the last lap; Schlam had to push his silent machine across the line to qualify as a finisher.

The third heat was between the Englishman Roger Frogley (very popular with the crowd at King's Oak, where he had made his speedway debut at that inaugural meeting only four months earlier) on his 500cc Rudge Whitworth and Australian Charlie Datson (500cc Douglas), who was the world record-holder for the 500cc half-mile dirt track. The crowd went wild as Frogley led the Aussie for the first two laps, but Datson was in trouble, his machine smoking badly and running erratically. However, when the engine cleared he set off after Frogley at such a pace that the Englishman's quarter-lap advantage had soon almost disappeared. If the race had lasted a half-lap longer Datson would certainly have won, but Frogley was still ahead, by a bare five yards, as he crossed the finishing line.

Various supporting races took place before the final, including a sidecar event which featured the path racing talents of Fred Brackpool and Gordon Norchi, Brackpool emerging the winner. Then came the final, which turned out to be less exciting than had been expected, with just Frogley and Wills lined up against Schlam, the lone Australian. When Schlam's engine cut on lap 2 it was left to Frogley to lead Wills home across the line.

The meeting as a whole, however, had been a great success, despite the weather. The excellent results by the English riders had delighted the crowd, of course, but to put things in perspective, the wet conditions had suited them far more than the Australians, who did not race at home in the wet.

A few alterations were made after the experience of this inaugural Crystal Palace meeting. It had become apparent that marshals armed with rakes could not hope to smooth out the track between races unaided in a reasonable time, so a tractor which towed three lengths of railway line at a 45-degree angle was introduced to smooth the ruts and speed the time between races. Also, the pits area was covered to give the riders some protection from rain while they worked on their bikes or waited for their next race.

Speedway meetings at the Palace then took a regular form, beginning with a parade of track officials dressed in white coats, the track rakers in orange and black, then those ever dependable stalwarts of the St John Ambulance Brigade. Music would blare from the loudspeakers and the riders would also be paraded in front of their cheering fans before the racing began.

During that first season, the racing was run on an individual match race basis, but in 1929 it was decided by the promoters of the many tracks operating throughout the country to form a league and have team racing. A Southern Inter-Track League was formed consisting of eight London teams – Crystal Palace, Stamford Bridge, Wembley, West Ham, White City, Harringay, Lea Bridge and Wimbledon. Southampton, Coventry and Birmingham also became big areas of speedway activity.

The still familiar 3-2-1-0 points-scoring system for each heat was introduced at this time, and as inter-team rivalry developed Crystal Palace fans were encouraged to support 'their' team, The Glaziers, who for 1929 were captained by Triss Sharp and consisted of George Lovick, Brian Donkin, Arthur Willimott, Joe Francis, Alf Sawford and Jack Barrett. That year, The Glaziers finished fourth in the league (Stamford Bridge were the champions).

Soon, supporters' clubs sprang up and team regalia and badges were being sold widely. Some 30,000 people joined the club at Crystal Palace, members not only being charged reduced admission fees, but also being able to buy such things as riders' photographs (2d, or 4d with an autograph), flags, ties, and vanity and cigarette cases, all decorated with The Glaziers badges or finished in the orange and black team colours. A couple of really keen supporters even managed to acquire the bell from the top of the turnstile at the Penge entrance to ring support to the team – this must have made the riders feel really at home at away matches!

Mockford and Smith tried various other entertainments to add interest to their meetings. Sidecar speedway proved very popular until 1930, the antics of the passengers always being very amusing, but most of those taking part were also path racing competitors and found it hard to fit in both

A reproduction of the programme issued for the meeting promoted in April 1931 by London Motor Sports Ltd for a Southern League speedway match between the Crystal Palace and Southampton teams.

The Crystal Palace speedway team for 1933 comprising, from the left: Triss Sharp, Joe Francis, Nobby Key, Fred Mockford (managing director), Ron Johnson, Tom Farndon, Harry Shepherd and George Newton.

When speedway came to Crystal Palace it quickly developed a devoted following and The Glaziers usually battled with the visiting team against a background of packed spectator terraces.

forms of the sport, so a lack of riders eventually brought it to a halt. Motorcycle football and sidecar polo on the football pitch were also tried, but it was always difficult to find suitable opposing teams despite the fact that the crowd found the football in particular very entertaining. Even horse racing was tried in 1928, with experienced jockeys riding heats and a final, speedway fashion. Since no betting was permitted, the interest soon waned.

Midget cars were also raced, but perhaps surprisingly did not provide much crowd appeal and also proved very expensive for the competitors. The best known drivers were Walter Mackereth and C S Dellow, with international competition provided by Frenchman Jean Reville and one Spike Rhiando, English-domiciled but variously reported as hailing from Mexico or Canada. Another keen Frenchman at the Palace was Ive de Lathe, who used to commute regularly from Paris to ride in the two-wheel events.

During the 1930 season, The Glaziers were cheered on to seventh place in the league. The team, now comprising Triss Sharp, Roger Frogley, Wally Lloyd, Joe Francis, Clem Mitchell, 'Shep' Shepherd and Australian Ron Johnston, were always heartened to see the fans with their orange and black scarves, hats and rosettes filling the stands.

Many of the best known riders of the day competed at the Palace, and among them was Fay Taylour, the top woman motorcycle racer. She began her speedway career in 1928 after spectating at the second Crystal Palace event. Dusting down her old AJS, she arrived for practice the following Friday. She fell off twice, but when Fred Mockford asked her, 'What do you think of speedway?' the reply was, 'Can I send a telegram from here?' 'Of course,' said the promoter. 'Well, send this,' said Fay: 'Butcher, Marine Parade, Douglas, Isle of Man. Please cancel room, not coming. Fay Taylour.' Mystified, Mockford asked what she meant. 'It means,' replied the lady rider, 'I don't want to watch any Isle of Man racing when I can come down here and practise every day.' Fred Mockford duly signed her up and a match race between Fay and Ron Johnston was included for the following meeting. In 1930, however, the ACU banned females from motorcycle sport following an accident at a speedway meeting when a woman fell from her machine and received severe chest injuries. Fay Taylour campaigned to get the ban reversed but without success, and the crowds were disappointed that 'The Cinders Queen' could not race again.

Many other notable names from the world of speedway competed at Crystal Palace. They included Joe Francis, who had a long career with The Glaziers and was also picked for the England international team. He became managing director of Brands Hatch Stadium Ltd in 1947, was instrumental in laying the hard surface to replace the original grass track there, and helped the 500 Club to get car racing started at the Kent venue. Ron Johnston was one of the original group of Australians who came over to introduce speedway in 1928 and he stayed to race in England until an accident confined him to a wheelchair in 1950. He had lost two fingers in a previous track mishap when he got them caught in the chain of his machine. Although born in Scotland, Ron had lived in Australia since his childhood, so he returned there after his serious crash. Roger Frogley and his brother 'Buster' (Arthur) became

Palace favourites. They developed their own 'Frogley Specials' based on Rudge dirt-trackers, racing and selling these machines with great success. Tom Farndon secured the title of Stars Riders Champion (forerunner of the World championship) in 1933. Favourite to win again in 1935, he was involved in a bad accident the evening before the final and, tragically, died 48 hours later without regaining consciousness. Triss Sharp, a South Croydon motor dealer, was the first Palace captain and liked by the fans for his distinctive leg-trailing style (most riders adopted the leg-forward cornering stance introduced by the Australians). Another 'name' was Arthur Willimott whose career was cut short when, like Johnston, he lost his fingers in an accident. Apart from Fay Taylour, four other ladies competed regularly at the Palace, though not quite with her degree of success; Eva Asquith, who eventually rode for Leeds, Dot Cowley, Babs Nield and Vera Hole.

Fred Mockford, always enterprising and by now gaining a reputation as the greatest speedway promoter of the time, had never been satisfied with the starting procedure for the early races. At first, the bikes were push-started by energetic track marshals, but seldom did all riders in a heat get away cleanly together. Rolling starts did not improve the situation much, so clutch starts were introduced in 1930. Still not happy, Mockford got together with Palace rider Harry Shepherd and in 1933 came up with the starting gate. Originally hand operated, then electrically powered, it was soon universally adopted by speedway tracks as the fairest way of starting a race.

The 500 Guinea Trophy donated for path racing by the Trustees was subsequently used for dirt-track competitions and became the Crystal Palace Track Trophy, the prize for an individual riders' championship. At first the fastest 12 team members contested it, later 16 riders were included in the competition. To be eligible, a rider had to have won a race at the Palace at more than 40mph. Triss Sharp became the first holder, in 1929, and in 1934, when the competition ceased, Tom Farndon was the winner. Farndon's name is also in the record books for the fastest lap of all time at Crystal Palace speedway, achieving 49.7mph. Harry Shepherd holds the record as the first rider to complete three laps from a standing start in less than a minute, receiving a trophy and cheque from a keen fan to mark the feat.

The Glaziers carried on racing throughout the early 1930s, finishing fourth in the Southern League in 1931, third in the 1932 NPA Trophy and, their best placing, second in 1932 when the competition was expanded to form the National League. In 1933 they were fourth.

They contested the 1934 National League, but by then interest in speedway was beginning to wane. As attendances and gate money decreased, the rent and rates on the track rose. To try to win back some of the crowds, Mockford asked if he could install floodlights and promote evening races but the Trustees turned the idea down. When the fees payable to the Trustees reached nearly £1,000 per week, Mockford decided to move the entire team the few miles to New Cross and begin again there. The 'Crystal Palace/New Cross' team finished third in the League that year, and the weeds began to appear through the cinders at the Palace oval.

Crystal Palace had seen many marvellous speedway races.

It was reported that on Easter Monday 1930 a total of 71,311 people had flocked into the park, many just to watch the speedway. In its heyday it could attract visitors from all over South East London and it became one of the capital's major entertainment centres.

The Palace had also played host to three international 'Speedway Tests'. On June 27, 1931, teams representing England and Australia met there in front of a huge crowd: England won the event with 55 points to the visitors' 37 and Eric Langton was the hero of the day, scoring 12 of those points. On August 6, 1932, Australia gained revenge in what *The Motor Cycle* called the 'Greatest Speedway Test Match of All Time'. With another very big crowd, in glorious weather, the match was a cliff-hanger, and the outcome all depended on the final heat. Ron Johnston led the riders home to clinch it for the Aussies, but Frank Varey put up a gallant chase only to have his back tyre burst. The third time the 'Test' came to the Palace was on July 29, 1933, when the result was even closer, England under their captain Ginger Lees scoring 63½ points, one more than the Australians.

Towards the end of 1937 work began on clearing the weeds and rubbish from the track, for Crystal Palace speedway was to be revived. A Second Division had been formed: the idea was that teams of novice and younger 'up-and-coming' riders should compete, but this was soon changed and more experienced competitors were allowed to take part. In 1938 the reborn Crystal Palace, with a new promoter and new riders, began its campaign in this new league. Their captain was Les Trim, who though very experienced had never quite made it into the big-time, and other riders were Les Gregory, Bob Lovell, Vic Weir, Keith Harvey, Lloyd Goffe, Archie Windmill, Geoff Dykes, Mick Mitchell and George Gower.

Somehow this new team couldn't quite recapture the spirit of the old one, and the crowds were never quite so big. With only 10 teams participating in the Second Division, the competition was never as tough as in the big league. Nevertheless, many exciting meetings were held at the Palace, and a new supporters' club was formed among the fans who attended.

The end for Crystal Palace speedway came as the war clouds of 1939 darkened. The track was used briefly for some races to entertain the troops in 1940, but after that the War Department took over and the speedway oval became a tank park. But although both path racing and speedway were now finished, the park had already been echoing to a different engine note and motor sport at Crystal Palace was entering the next stage in its development.

One of the less successful motor sports promotions at Crystal Palace during the Thirties was midget car racing, small fields and poor spectator support causing it to be abandoned after less than a season.

CHAPTER 4

A purpose-built road-racing track

Cars and motorcycles on 2 miles of tarmac, 1935 to 1939

With the demise of path racing and The Glaziers' move to New Cross Speedway, the two tracks at Crystal Palace lay silent and unused. Many of the other varied events once held in the park had also ceased, including the motor boat races on the North Tower Lake, and in the mid-1930s the future of the whole site looked bleak. A few people attended the organ recitals and concerts held in the Palace itself, but Paxton's great glasshouse was otherwise filled with rather dusty and run-down exhibits. New attractions were clearly needed if the crowds were to return to the once very popular venue.

Towards the end of 1935 rumours in the motor sporting press began to tell of a 'Donington for London'. Sir Henry Buckland, general manager of the Trustees, had decided that as the Palace had proved so popular in the past with motor sport enthusiasts, a proper road racing circuit within the grounds might well bring the crowds back. He was prepared to go ahead with the project providing the response from the organizing clubs was favourable. His proposal was to hold about 10 meetings a year, six for motorcycles and four for cars. The planned course would roughly follow the perimeter of the park but would have a tight 'inner circuit' too, and would be two or two and a quarter miles in length. Clubs were urged to give their support to these ambitious plans, and the future for motor sport at Crystal Palace began to look rosier.

Almost a year passed without further news of the project. The public must have wondered if the proposals had foundered, but a lot had been happening behind the scenes. Harry Edwards of the International Road Racing Club had been very interested to hear about the plans. He was also secretary of the British Racing Drivers' Club and an active member of the South Eastern Centre of the Auto-Cycle Union, and had support from racing driver W G (Bill) Everitt and the Hon G G R Rodd. The three men held detailed discussions with Sir Henry Buckland and the Trustees, and together they prepared a final plan for the track and associated amenities. The design was drawn up by the appointed architect, C L Clayton, who had been behind a similar but unsuccessful scheme to build a road racing circuit in Brighton.

The track that Clayton had designed was 30ft wide except at the start/finish line where it was increased to 50ft. The grid was on Stadium Straight which ran for some 500yds with the sports ground and speedway track to the right, so that the Speedway Bank gave spectators a good vantage point. A subway beneath Stadium Straight would give access to the infield. The track turned right into Ramp Bend, passing under Ramp Bridge which also led to the infield and speedway track parking areas for competitors and spectators. The road then began a steady climb for some 350yds through the very twisty sections of the Anerley Ramp and Maxim Rise, passing the Low Level Railway Station to the left, where the Road Racing Club had its offices, under the low level bridge and through the Alley to a 90-degree right-hand bend, South Tower Corner. A replica of the Canadian Parliament building stood on the inside of the corner. South Tower, according to contemporary publicity, was 'super-elevated', enabling cars to exit onto Terrace Straight at high speed. This section, almost half a mile long, was the fastest part of the circuit and it was confidently expected that the fastest competitors of the day would reach about 135mph. As planned, this straight would have been in the shadow of the Crystal Palace itself, the Lower Terrace providing an excellent viewpoint, with the Terrace Bridge halfway down the straight. A slight left-hand kink followed, then competitors would need to be braking hard for one of the trickiest places, North Tower Crescent, a long right-hander which led into perhaps the prettiest part of the circuit, The Glade, an avenue of trees and rhododendron bushes. The back gardens of the residents of Crystal Palace Park Road adjoined the track here – great if you enjoyed motor racing! Spectators were denied access to this area, which was a pity as the sight of racing through the trees and shrubs here on a sunny day was one of the most attractive on any track. Downhill from The Glade the road went into a tight right-

Desolation. The morning after the big fire on November 30, 1936, which gutted the Crystal Palace and left little but part of the shell and the two towers remaining. But three days later the first turf was cut to mark the beginning of a new era in motor sports at The Palace with the construction of a purpose-built road circuit.

hander at Fisherman's Bend, with the Intermediate Lake on the inside to catch out the unwary. A slight flick to the left and a sharp right made up the tricky S-bend of Fisherman's Corner, and the road circuit now began to follow roughly the course of the old path-racing track, though in the reverse direction. Climbing again up Fisherman's Rise with the Maze and Maze Car Park to the left and a pond to the right, the track arrived at the slowest corner, Pond Hairpin (Rockhills Hairpin in path-racing days). A sweeping downhill section running roughly parallel to Terrace Straight brought the competitor to Big Tree Bend, named because of the very large tree which grew on the inside of the course: it was a tricky corner with Cedar Pond on the outside just at the exit from the curve. Down New Zealand Hill (the replica government building still stood to the right) and under the bridge brought you into Stadium Dip, which, following the fast descent, proved to be a spectacular viewing point, before skirting the sports ground through Stadium Curve, overlooked by another popular vantage

point for spectators on Cascade Bank, and back onto Stadium Straight, crossing the start/finish line in front of the grandstand, press stand, and boxes for the announcers, timekeepers and director.

Three scoreboards were to be installed, one at North Tower, one on New Zealand Hill and one near the paddock at Anerley Ramp. A Tannoy public address system was also on the plan, as were various cafes and refreshment kiosks. It was envisaged too that the facilities inside the Crystal Palace would be used by race spectators, but that was not to be.

Mr Clayton confidently guaranteed the circuit length to be 2 miles (within 3 inches!) and all the interested parties agreed that the plans were ideal. Civil engineers W & C French, of Buckhurst Hill, Essex, were contracted to build the track and bridges, while Bituminous Surfacing Ltd, of London and Manchester, were to surface the road with 'Panamac', which they proudly advertised as durable, dependable and non-skid. On Thursday, December 3, 1936, the first turf was cut and work began on turning the dream

Racing past the back door. Rayson's Maserati leads Hanson's Maserati and Cotton's Riley through Fisherman's Bend during the first car race meeting in 1937. The new era of motor and motorcycle racing, however, did not get the unanimous approval of the residents of Crystal Palace Park Road.

A map of the 2-miles circuit incorporating the slow inner loop after Fisherman's Bend, which would be deleted when the circuit was reopened for racing after World War 2, thereby reducing the lap length to 1.39 miles.

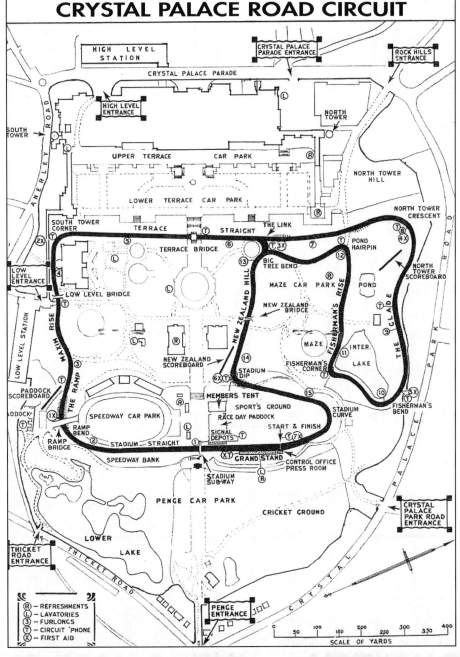

CRYSTAL PALACE ROAD CIRCUIT

of road racing in London into reality. It began, though, in the shadow of a totally unforeseen disaster.

Three days earlier, on Monday, November 30, 1936, a security man checking the Crystal Palace building during the early evening noticed a small fire. He alerted his fellow security officers and an attempt was made to quell the blaze but it developed beyond their control so the fire station at Penge was called. Their fire appliances were quickly at the scene, but so rapid was the spread of fire that the chief officer realized additional help was needed and fire crews were called in from all over the South London, Croydon and Sutton areas. The iron and glass structure itself might have been fairly fire-resistant but the wooden floors and the accumulated exhibits inside burned fiercely. As the flames lit up the darkening autumnal sky and news of the great fire was broadcast on the radio, crowds began to gather to witness the scene.

At the height of the fire over 60 engines were at the Palace and the police were stopping traffic half a mile away to allow the fire fighters easy access. Efforts to quench the flames were hampered by lack of water pressure at the top of the hill so hoses were used to take water from the North Tower boating lake, the reservoir and the lakes near the Penge entrance, all of which were quickly drained as the inferno worsened. The great areas of glass were by now melting and molten glass ran down Anerley Hill and Crystal Palace Parade like volcanic lava. It solidified in the tracks of the tramway, putting the trams out of action for a while. As the grand old building burned out of control all that night the orange glow in the sky could be seen all over South London.

By dawn the fire was out but Joseph Paxton's Crystal Palace was no more. All that remained was the twisted iron skeleton, blackened and bent by the intense heat, lying between the twin North and South Towers which the fire brigade had managed, almost miraculously, to save. Another miracle was that no-one had been hurt in the inferno.

Scrap metal was all that could be salvaged from the Palace, and the remains were cut up and shipped to Krupps in Essen, perhaps eventually by a terrible irony to form parts of the bombers or the deadly cargo they would be dropping on London during the Blitz just four years later. Lloyds insurance promptly paid out £110,000 (a far more formidable sum in 1936 than it sounds today) and the site was cleared. The once proud landmark of South London and one of the great symbols of Victorian achievement was gone.

But the park remained and, without the Crystal Palace and many of the former amenities, replacement attractions were needed urgently, so work on the racing circuit proceeded with all speed. During the winter of 1936–37 the track quickly took shape and in early April it was complete. To have built the circuit in about five months, in the poor weather and short daylight of winter, was a considerable feat. The winter had been the wettest for a century, too, and W & C French had been badly hampered by mudslides as they excavated the foundations for the road.

Despite these problems, the contractors had done an excellent job, and the Crystal Palace Road Racing Circuit was greeted with great enthusiasm by the press, competitors and spectators alike. In his 'On Four Winds' column in *The Motor Cycle*, 'Nitor' described part of the new course as 'resembling a miniature Nürburgring' and said 'The Palace grounds have been transformed. . . the true rider will be in his element. . . the non-skid surface is as smooth as the proverbial billiard ball.' The top British racing driver of the 1930s, Richard Seaman, signed up to drive for the mighty Mercedes-Benz works team in 1937, was another who relished the new prospect, having followed the construction work with great interest and visited the circuit on a number of occasions. In an introduction for the programme of the first meeting, he wrote, 'The design of the circuit, with straights that are not too long, gradual and sharp bends, climbs and descents, gives the sport a condensed circuit employing practically every hazard to be encountered on Continental courses, and it is hoped that British manufacturers, with such an excellent testing ground at their disposal, will be encouraged to build racing cars to

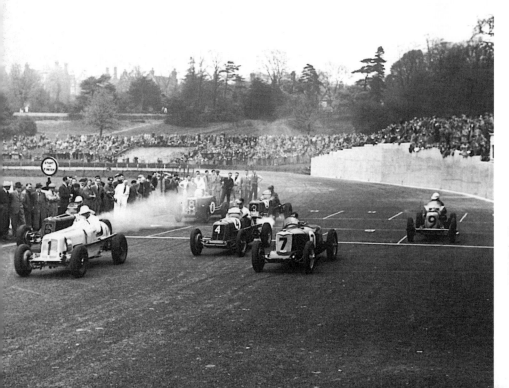

Heat 1 of the Coronation Trophy race in April 1937. The ERA of Scribbans (car 1) makes a good start ahead of Maclure's Riley (7) and the ERAs of Fairfield (6) and Rayson (4).

Spectators were quick to discover that the raised terraces overlooking Ramp Bend provided one of the best vantage points alongside the new circuit.

A view across the infield from the start-finish straight showing the part of New Zealand Hill preceding the left-handed Stadium Dip, and in the background the empty shell of what used to be a magnificent building.

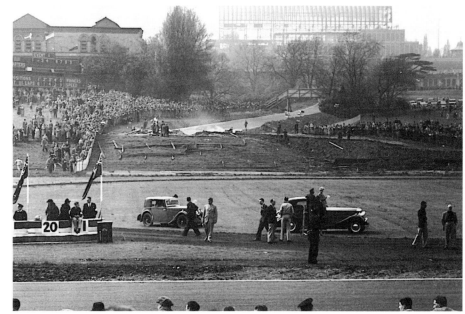

Overlooking Stadium Curve, the final bend of the circuit approaching the start-finish line, with the main grandstand on the left and the paddock area on the right.

Raymond Mays and his ERA at the first meeting in 1937 with the North Tower dominating the skyline. Along with its partner, the South Tower, it would provide a useful navigational aid for the Luftwaffe heading for South London during the early days of World War 2 until both structures were dynamited.

rival the pre-eminent Continental machines.'

The track did indeed resemble a Continental road circuit as it wound its way through the trees of the park and between the decaying replica government buildings left from the 1911 Empire Exhibition. The Road Racing Club were very proud of it, calling it 'paramount' and hoping it would become 'the Mecca of the sport in this country'.

A fixture list for 1937 had been drawn up, with April 24 named as the date for the first meeting to be held on the new Crystal Palace circuit. Mecca Cafes Ltd would provide 'light refreshment', luncheons were available in the North Tower Restaurant, and uniformed attendants would sell programmes. A special one-shilling return train fare from Victoria or London Bridge would take the spectator to the Low Level station, or he could choose from nine different bus and trolley-bus services to get him to one of the entrances. Half a crown (two shillings and sixpence) would get an adult into a car race meeting – for children and boy scouts it was only one shilling! Anyone lucky enough to have a car could park it at the Terrace car park also for 'two-and-six' or, for the wealthy, the Penge car park would cost five shillings (25p). Admission to motorcycle meetings would cost two shillings for adults, one shilling for children and parking. There was no need for advanced booking because of the 'unlimited accommodation within the Crystal Palace Park'.

Once inside, the spectator would find that, according to the Road Racing Club's publicity, 'The Crystal Palace Circuit is a typical modern highway, 2 miles in length and 30 feet wide. . . spectators are, by means of five bridges and a subway, able to move freely around practically every section of the circuit during racing, a facility not offered to the same degree at any other racing circuit.' Marshals had been appointed, many of them members of the Carshalton MCC, and given duties on the circuit, in the paddock, running the scoreboards or helping to control spectators. Messrs Antifyre Ltd provided the necessary fire precautions and St John Ambulance workers were in attendance. Earl Howe and Sir Algernon Guinness were stewards, with Roland King-Farlow as chief timekeeper, and observers included John Eason Gibson and Major Goldie Gardner. H R Godfrey was scrutineer, Harry Edwards clerk of the course and G Denton provided the commentary. All officials were rewarded with a free lunch, either in the press room or the Chalet restaurant which adjoined the paddock.

With practice set for Thursday, April 22, 1937, the contractors had to work very hard to get the circuit ready in time. Finishing touches were still required when that day arrived, and building equipment still littered the park, but the track was finished and enough facilities were available for the meeting to go ahead. Twenty cars had been entered for the Coronation Trophy – 1937 was the year of the crowning of King George VI.

On the entry list were six ERAs, the works cars of Raymond Mays and Pat Fairfield and four privately owned cars to be driven by Dennis Scribbans, Ian Connell, Arthur Dobson and Peter Whitehead. Against the English cars were three Maseratis, Charlie Brackenbury in a 4CM and the 6CMs of Robin Hanson and Austin Dobson. Aubrey Esson-Scott entered his modified Bugatti, Bill Humphreys and Reg Parnell had MGs, Percy Maclure, bandleader Billy Cotton and former motorcyclist Freddy Dixon had all entered Rileys, Cotton's to be driven by 'Wilkie' Wilkinson, and a modified Riley was entered by R W Appleton. The Hon Peter Aitken and A M C Jameson had Frazer Nashes and the entry was completed by the two Altas of A G Sinclair and P F Jucker.

Races at the existing British circuits, Brooklands and Donington, were usually run over a long distance, 200 to 500 miles, but the organizers decided to run Palace races as the French and Italians did, with two qualifying heats and a final. They felt that shorter races would provide the spectators with more interest and suit the nature of the track better, ensuring close racing throughout.

Large crowds attended the practice sessions and watched the ERAs set the fastest times. Onlookers and competitors alike were full of enthusiasm for the new circuit and eager for the racing proper to commence. The Road Racing Club were confident that they could live up to their slogan, 'The Sign of Good Racing'. Prizes on offer were £50 for a heat win and £150 for the final plus the handsome bronze Coronation Trophy depicting a javelin thrower, presented by Jack Barclay. Good racing seemed assured.

Saturday, April 24, saw people flocking to the Crystal Palace to experience first hand the thrill of motor racing in the capital city, and there was an atmosphere of great excitement as the cars lined up for the first 20-lap heat. From pole position, car number 1, the white ERA of Dennis Scribbans, headed the field with the works ERA of Pat Fairfield in pursuit, followed by Brackenbury (Maserati), Maclure (Riley), Humphreys (MG), Connell (ERA) and Aitken (Frazer Nash). Soon, Fairfield took the lead and Scribbans dropped back, the close, cut-and-thrust racing keeping the spectators excited lap after lap. Fairfield came home the winner of the first event on the new British circuit, beating the Maserati of Brackenbury by just over a minute, with Aitken's Frazer Nash third and Maclure's Riley fourth. The winner's average speed was 52.63mph. In the second heat, ERAs finished first, second and third, Raymond Mays leading home Dobson and Whitehead, with Wilkie Wilkinson fourth in Billy Cotton's Riley.

The final was over 30 laps (60 miles), and it was Dobson who led off the line, with Fairfield, Mays and Whitehead behind. After the ERA quartet came Brackenbury's Maserati, followed by Wilkinson (Riley), Hanson (Maserati), Maclure (Riley) and Aitken (Frazer Nash). Mays displaced Fairfield to take second on lap 2 and both cars tailed the leader very closely, taking Dobson and relegating him to third on lap 3. By the seventh lap Fairfield was in the lead and Mays was in trouble, stopping soon after. By half distance the order was Fairfield, Dobson, Whitehead and Hanson (Maserati). The two ERAs at the front led convincingly and were first and second across the line, but Whitehead had dropped back by the finish, allowing Hanson's Maserati to take third from Maclure's Riley in

fourth place. Fairfield won by some 59 seconds, his winning time being 1hr 7min 8.8sec, an average speed of 53.77mph. He also set fastest lap and the first lap record with a time of 2min 12sec, an average of 54.59mph.

The racing had proved very exciting – almost too exciting for some, as Aubrey Esson-Scott had caused a moment or two of panic among press men watching from the bottom of New Zealand Hill when he arrived at Stadium Dip too fast, spun his Bugatti and crashed backwards over the earth bank which was their vantage point! Wilkie Wilkinson was another driver in trouble; he was lying fifth when a con-rod in the Riley engine let go, punching a hole in the sump and causing him to hit the bank just after Stadium Dip. Generally, though, drivers and spectators seemed very pleased with the day's events. What those local residents not interested in racing thought of it all, finding the peace of their Saturday afternoon shattered by the proceedings at the Palace, is another matter.

Three weeks later, the peace in SE19 was shattered again when the motorcycle racers converged on the Palace. Many people felt the twists and turns of the track would suit the bikes more than the cars, and some predicted that the two-wheelers would lap faster than the four-wheelers. Many of the top riders had entered and once again large crowds arrived to witness the spectacle.

Events began at 3pm and the audience was first treated to a demonstration run by Eric Fernihough, fresh from some record-breaking runs in Hungary on a streamlined, highly modified JAP-powered Brough Superior which was the fastest bike in the world at the time. In the racing that followed, the 60-mile Junior Coronation Grand Prix produced an exciting tussle between H Watson (Velocette), George Rowley (AJS), Harold Daniell (Norton) and the Velocettes of E A Mellors and H W Antell.

As Watson and Rowley diced for the lead, all eyes were on Maurice Cann (Norton) and Ginger Woods (Excelsior), who were rapidly hauling in the leaders. By the fifth lap, Cann had taken the lead from Daniell and Woods. But

Aubrey Esson-Scott's Bugatti came to grief at the opening meeting, spinning and ending up on top of the bank on the outside of Stadium Dip with a crumpled tail and what appears to be an acute case of rear-wheel steering.

Ginger fell from his mount first at Big Tree Bend, then again a short time later, and although he remounted each time, he fell back through the field. Other riders too found the twisting track rather tricky and ended up on the floor. At the front, Cann continued to lead from Daniell and Rowley. Kenneth Bills (Norton) moved into fourth, holding the position despite a fall, and this was the order as they crossed the finishing line. Cann's winning speed was 53.15mph.

The Coronation Sidecar race had only six entrants and was not very exciting. The main amusement for the fans came when Jack Surtees' Norton outfit hit the bank at Stadium Curve, depositing both rider and passenger on their backs, before continuing on its way across the grass verge, hitting the Secretary of the Meeting's car and neatly removing a door, then colliding with a fire tender! The racing was a flag-to-flag win for A H Horton (Norton) from the similar outfits of B Ducker and F E Ratcliffe, after W Graham's AJS had retired from second place.

The main race of the day, the Senior Coronation Grand Prix, was led initially by M D Whitworth (Triumph) but after two laps both Harold Daniell (Norton) and J M West (Ariel) had passed him. Stanley Woods on his Velocette steadily moved through the field, much to the excitement of the spectators, moving up to sixth place by lap 10; soon he was scrapping with West for second place which he finally took. Then West retook Woods and set off in pursuit of the flying Daniell, but the leader was lapping at around 54mph and West could make no headway despite trying very hard – too hard in fact, for in the closing stages he took a tumble, remounting quickly but letting Woods through into second place.

Somewhat surprisingly, in spite of the fine performance by Daniell, the fastest lap of the day had been set by Maurice Cann in the Junior race and his speed, 55.13mph, was indeed slightly faster than Pat Fairfield's lap in the ERA, confirming the predictions of those who had suggested before the event that the bikes would prove faster than the cars on this circuit.

On Saturday, June 12, 1937, the Road Racing Club, really living up to its name as an organizer of all types of racing on wheels, promoted the 100-kilometre International Cup race for professional cyclists. Though cycle racing was very popular on the Continent, where races were often held on public roads, it did not have such a wide following in the UK. Nevertheless, many people were attracted to the event which featured some of the top European riders of the day including Maurice Richard of France, Jean Aerts and G Daneels of Belgium and Grundahl Hansen from Denmark.

Work on the circuit was continuing apace. The muddy earth safety banks had been sown with grass seed and the debris left by construction work cleared. New refreshment kiosks and facilities to replace those destroyed in the fire the previous year had been built, and the Road Racing Club had many new ideas to try, some of them received when spectators were asked to send in criticisms and suggestions for improvements.

Some of these improvements were in evidence on July 17 when the London Grand Prix was held, with a motorcycle sidecar race as the supporting event. It was at this meeting that Bira made his first appearance at Crystal Palace, driving the famous ERA R2B called Romulus.

'B. Bira' was the name adopted by Prince Birabongse of Siam, who had proved an extremely skilled racing driver. He and his cousin and team manager Prince Chula Chakrabongse were well known in English society, and he was hailed as a hero in his native Siam (now Thailand).

Another visitor was Major Goldie Gardner, who gave the crowd a demonstration lap in his record-breaking MG Magnette, receiving a standing ovation. The car was then put on show in the paddock behind a wooden fence, causing small boys to gaze open-mouthed in wonder.

Raymond Mays took the flag in the first heat, leading home Connell, Maclure and Aitken. Bira won Heat 2, in the process setting a new lap record at 56.47mph. Dobson (ERA) was second from Parnell (MG) and Hanson (Maserati). Bira underlined his skill by going on to win the final, completing the 15 laps in 33min 3.7sec and finishing just over a minute ahead of Ian Connell (ERA), with Percy Maclure's Riley third and Parnell's MG fourth. Dobson took the lead at one stage during the race, but crashed out of contention after a rare mistake. Also at this meeting were the little 750cc works Austin Seven single-seaters, and these diminutive racers thrilled the crowd with their nimble cornering, being ideally suited to the short straights and twists and turns of the Palace circuit.

On August 14 a 'Grand Composite Meeting' was held, with the Crystal Palace Cup for cars, The Crystal Palace Trophy for motorcycles and the Crystal Palace Plate for amateur cyclists. The entry list contained well known names in each sport, and for 2s 6d admission the spectators were promised a full programme of racing. Although the weather was unkind that day, the variety on offer clearly had a strong appeal and nearly 4,000 people braved the rain. At 3pm the 45 cyclists set off for a five-lap race, run in the opposite direction to the cars and motorcycles to provide a long straight for the anticipated sprint finish. Half-way through the race, the rain stopped and the skies cleared a little. The competitors made a fine sight in their colourful jerseys as they snaked round the circuit, and their speed increased as the weather lifted, the first lap record for cyclists being set at an impressive 23.8mph.

The track remained wet and slippery throughout, odd showers continuing to fall, and quite a few motorcyclists came to grief in the subsequent events, particularly at Fisherman's Bend which was extra treacherous. The race for solo bikes was a handicap, with the scratch riders including Harold Daniell, J M West and T E Arter preceded from the start by a group with 10 seconds advantage and another with five seconds. In front of everyone else was A H Castle on a Grindlay Peerless who was given a few extra seconds on the rest of the 31 riders, and he managed to hang on to his lead for a lap or two before the faster men engulfed him. After two laps Daniell had taken the lead, with Maurice Cann (Norton) and A R Foster (AJS) breathing down his neck. E J Cashman (Norton) was also charging, and took Cann for second place on lap 7, setting fastest lap of the day at 51.1mph. But on the next lap, Foster and Cann moved up to first and second places ahead of Daniell and Cashman, and it was Cann who finally got in front to win.

Then the sidecars came out for a five-lap, 10-mile race which produced a fierce scrap between A H Horton

It was the motorcycle racers' chance to sample the new Crystal Palace circuit for the first time a month after the first car meeting, and there was no shortage of entries for either of the two main events, the Junior and Senior Coronation Grands Prix.

Not so the Coronation Sidecar race, which drew just six entries and four finishers, including F E Ratcliffe, whose passenger is striving to bring the Norton combination's third wheel back in contact with the circuit.

Time for celebration. Harold Daniell, winner of the Senior Coronation Grand Prix, astride his Norton and flanked by Stanley Woods, whose Velocette finished second, and Jock West, who took a late tumble from his Ariel when chasing Daniell, but quickly remounted to finish third.

(Norton), G H Taylor (Ariel) and F E Ratcliffe (Norton), these three outfits eventually crossing the finishing line in that order. Behind the leaders, it was a race of numerous incidents: among other mishaps, the Norton of B H Kimberley overturned at one point and Jack Surtees had a nasty spill when the throttle on his Norton outfit stuck wide open on the approach to a corner.

In the 30-lap car race which rounded off the afternoon, the works Austin single-seaters appeared again, driven by Bert Hadley and Mrs Kay Petre. These tiny supercharged cars with their distinctive high-revving scream made a lasting impression on the spectators, particularly when Hadley took on the much bigger Maserati of Bira in a close-fought duel which was resolved when Bira went off the road and the little Austin carried on to win at a race average of 49.83mph. Bira recovered to take second place, and set the fastest lap at 2min 14.8sec, 53.50mph. Reg Parnell was third in his MG and Maclure (Riley) was fourth. At the end of the race the rain came down again, but the crowd went home well pleased with a day of entertaining variety and good racing.

On October 9, 1937, the Palace hosted its biggest event so far when the International Imperial Trophy Race was held. The BBC recognized the importance of the day and televised the meeting: it was the first ever TV outside broadcast of motor sport and they devoted much of that Saturday afternoon to it, this at a period when television was still in its infancy, very much a prerogative of the wealthy, and broadcasting was restricted to about four hours a day. The *Radio Times* gave notice of the event – 'the first International Road Race in London (by courtesy of the Road Racing Club) on the Crystal Palace Road Racing Circuit (conditions permitting).' Coverage began with 30 minutes at 2.25pm and further visits to the Palace were transmitted (live, no video recordings in 1937) at 3.15 and 3.45, with the final 45 minutes at 4.15. F J Findon, editor of *Light Car* magazine, provided the commentary and interviewed Dick Seaman, who also wrote the introduction to the programme, praising the efforts of the Road Racing Club in achieving so much in their first season at Crystal Palace. Although Mercedes were not competing in the event, Seaman gave a demonstration run in his silver 645bhp car, a sight to be remembered by many spectators at the meeting. By contrast, the Hon Peter Mitchell-Thomson had earlier demonstrated his Mercedes, the car which had won the Ballyslaughter Hill Climb in 1903.

The impressive entry for the Imperial Trophy comprised 21 cars, with a genuinely international element provided by three Scuderia Ambrosiana Maseratis for Count Trossi,

Kay Petre, one of Britain's most prominent and successful lady drivers prior to World War Two, tackles Stadium Dip in her Austin single-seater during the August 1937 meeting.

Richard Seaman, who wrote the introduction to the programme for the first meeting on the new Crystal Palace circuit in April 1937, returned to South London for the October meeting to demonstrate his Grand Prix Mercedes-Benz W125 prior to the final of the main event, the Imperial Trophy race.

Count Lurani and Luigi Villoresi. Maseratis were also to be driven by Hanson, Aitken and Hyde, and they were up against six ERAs for Mays, Dobson, Bira, Connell, Whitehead and Martin. The two works Austins were to be driven by Hadley and Goodacre. H Stuart Wilton and J H Smith had MGs, Brooke his MG-Riley, and the field was completed by Sinclair (Alta), Nash (Frazer Nash), Leitch (Bugatti) and Maclure's Riley, the only unsupercharged car entered. Pat Fairfield, hitherto a Palace regular, was tragically missing as he had been killed at Le Mans.

The race was to follow the now established Crystal Palace pattern of two heats and a final, and the cars were divided into three handicap classes, with the Austins, MGs, MG-Riley and Mays' ERA in Class A (though Mays was unable to start as his 1,100cc engine blew up in practice) and Class B consisting of the rest of the entry except for Hyde's eight-cylinder 3-litre Maserati which was alone on scratch. Class A received a 50-second start, Class B 10 seconds.

The remarkable Riley of Percy Maclure took the chequered flag in Heat 1, beating Dobson's ERA by almost a second, with Lurani third and Whitehead fourth. Trossi won the second heat with his Maserati, followed by Martin and Bira, with Charlie Goodacre's little Austin fourth. Twenty cars started the final, the biggest field yet assembled on the grid at Crystal Palace. The Imperial Trophy and £150 first prize was at stake, as well as the Jarvis Trophy for the fastest lap, with the added prestige of television coverage, and the race looked certain to be exciting. It really lived up to expectations, with Bira and Dobson duelling for the lead throughout the 15 laps, leaving the others behind. Running nose to tail, the two smashed Bira's earlier lap record, Dobson finally leaving it at 58.63mph, and they crossed the line 0.3sec apart with Bira just taking the honours. Goodacre's Austin was third, with Villoresi fourth in the Maserati. The crowd had been entertained to a magnificent motor race and the BBC had been provided with an excellent spectacle just a few miles from Big Ben, a fitting end to a very promising first season on the new circuit.

It was a first season which had shown clearly how popular motor racing could be in the capital city. At a time when car ownership was still confined largely to the well-to-do, Crystal Palace, with its ease of access, was bringing the sport to the average man in the street and helping to broaden the appeal of what had been a rich man's pastime. Even if some local residents did not share the enthusiasm of the spectators for the roar of the racing cars and bikes which filled their Saturday afternoons, the large crowds had proved to those in charge at the Palace that their faith in the project was justified and their investment had been worthwhile. It is worth remembering, too, that from the point of view of the British fan, Crystal Palace played a very significant role because it was one of only three road-racing venues on the mainland. Occasional street races were still held on the Isle of Man, in Ulster and in the Channel Islands, but the only other places where circuit racing was possible in this country in the 1930s were Brooklands and Donington. Silverstone, Brands Hatch and the smaller circuits which have fostered the fertile growth of club racing in the UK are a postwar phenomenon.

Over the winter of 1937–38 the Crystal Palace track was resurfaced to make it less slippery, and, despite the worsening political situation in Europe, plans were optimistically drawn up for the following season. For 1938, the Road Racing Club announced from their offices in Queen's Gate Terrace, Kensington, motorcycle races would be included at all the car race meetings at Crystal Palace, but cycle races were discontinued for a time. The calendar listed six meetings planned for the year, five car races with motorcycle support and one all-motorcycle meeting, the latter fixed for September 10. All the car races were designated as of international status, for foreign entries had proved to be a big attraction.

So the season began on April 2 with the Coronation Trophy meeting. For the car race, in two heats and a final, the entry was divided into handicap classes. For the 10-lap heats, cars under 1,100cc were given a minute's start, cars over 1,100cc up to 2,500cc had a 10-second advantage, and those over 2,500cc started from scratch. The final was 16 laps, and here the smallest cars had a 96-second advantage and the 1,100cc to 2,500cc class received 16 seconds. Once again £150 prize money would go to the winner of the final, and 20 drivers, including some of the hoped-for foreign competitors, were entered for the event.

In Heat 1 were Hadley's Austin, Bira and Connell in ERAs, Everitt and Brooke in MGs, Maclure's Riley, Aitken and Johnny Wakefield (of the Wakefield oil company, better known later by its brand name, Castrol) in six-cylinder Maseratis, and two Delahayes for Joseph Paul and James Willing. As was becoming the norm, Bira won, from Wakefield, Hadley and Maclure. Heat 2 involved Tony Rolt and Arthur Dobson in ERAs, George Abecassis in an Alta, two more Delahayes for Louis Gerard and John Snow, Robin Hanson in a lone Maserati, Charlie Dodson in an Austin, J H T Smith's MG, and R Featherstonhaugh who was driving Hans Ruesch's 3.8 Alfa Romeo as the owner was unavailable to race it himself. This time, Arthur Dobson was the winner, with Hanson second, Dodson third and Smith fourth.

Before the final came a five-lap motorcycle sidecar race, in which seven 500cc outfits were flagged away five seconds before four 600cc machines. After a close race, A H Horton was the winner by just a yard from F E Ratcliffe, followed by Jack Surtees, the first three on Nortons, with Eric Oliver (Oliver JAP) fourth.

The final produced another Bira/Dobson duel, with Bira equalling the Englishman's lap record, until Dobson was forced to drop back with mechanical problems. Bira won, while Dobson had another fierce scrap with Wakefield (Maserati), losing second place to the Italian car by half a length. Hadley came in fourth. Once more the crowd had seen some good racing, and the growing reputation of the Road Racing Club and Crystal Palace had been further enhanced by a radio commentary broadcast by the BBC World Service.

On May 21 a meeting for cars and motorcycles of all classes was held in bright spring sunshine and thousands attended. At 3.30pm, 34 mixed 350cc and 500cc solo bikes were flagged away, with Palace favourite Maurice Cann leading the field on his 350cc Norton before making a rare mistake and dropping the machine at Stadium Curve. He sprang to his feet and restarted in the middle of the snarling pack, but Kenneth Bills had now taken the lead on a 500cc Norton and was never seriously challenged. Behind him, though, W A Lampkin and H Watson on 350 Velocettes and N Croft and J Moore on 350 Nortons kept swopping places, with C G Murdock (350 Norton) and the irrepressible Cann catching them fast. By lap 11, the crowd were on their feet straining to see the action, for Maurice Cann had moved into third place between Croft and Murdock. They remained in each other's wheel tracks for three laps, and in a frantic last-corner effort at Stadium Curve, evidently quite undeterred by his earlier fall at the same bend, Cann rode round the outside of Murdock to snatch second place by a matter of inches. The winner, Bills, who had already crossed the line, was quite forgotten in all the excitement!

Only seven sidecars came to the line for the Sydenham Vase – almost reduced further when Jack Surtees' passenger went missing, arriving only just in time for the start. T F Pullin (Pullin Special) and Eric Oliver (Oliver JAP) were both left on the grid, eventually starting after the others had departed, and F E Ratcliffe was not allowed to start as he arrived at the line when the field was already halfway round the first lap. Horton crashed heavily when his Norton outfit was hit by another competitor. This left G H Taylor, B Ducker and Jack Surtees in charge at the front and all three had a turn at leading. Surtees eventually took the honours ahead of Ducker with C F Smith on another Norton third.

The final bike event of the day was a five-lap invitation race for the Sydenham Cup, and this saw Maurice Cann get his revenge on Kenneth Bills after the two had worked their way through the field from the handicap start. D Parkinson (350 Excelsior) had led at first from J M West (Ariel) and G E Rowley (AJS). Bills put up a valiant chase, just as Cann had in their earlier encounter, but was unable to catch the local favourite. Parkinson came home third.

The four-wheelers racing that day put on a fine show, competing for the Sydenham Trophy. The silver Alta of George Abecassis led initially and seemed certain of an untroubled victory until a spin almost put the car in the lake. J H (John) Smith inherited the lead and went on to win. Bira chased him hard and set the fastest lap in the process at 2min 8.7sec (56.5mph). Maclure (Riley) was third, Rolt (ERA) fourth and Hanson (Maserati) fifth. These composite meetings, bikes and cars racing on the same day, were becoming very popular with the Crystal Palace crowd: as well as the variety, the relatively short races made for close competition and were easy to follow, providing a lot of entertainment value.

The next meeting on the calendar was the London Grand Prix. In those prewar days before the advent of the drivers' World Championship and the evolution of the tightly controlled and heavily commercialized circus which Formula 1 motor racing has become today, the title 'Grand Prix' did not of course imply that the race was part of any world series. The factory Mercedes-Benz team, sweeping all before them on the international scene, were not about to be unleashed in the confines of the Crystal Palace Park. Nevertheless, the races at the Palace had acquired enough of a reputation to draw a genuinely international entry: there were plenty of people unable to match the resources of the state-sponsored German

'silver arrows' who still wanted to compete and the greater variety and unpredictability of this older and less unrelentingly professional kind of racing went a long way to compensate for anything it might have lacked in sheer spectacle.

Entries secured by the Road Racing Club for the meeting on June 25, 1938 included, in addition to most of the regular Palace protagonists, two pale blue Simca Fiats, these French cars being driven by Anne Itier and Amedee Gordini, later to become a notable racing car constructor in his own right. With Bira and Dobson winning their respective heats, the crowd anticipated another showdown between the two ERA drivers, and they were not disappointed. After 16 laps, Bira took the chequered flag some 14 seconds ahead of Dobson, with Cuddon-Fletcher (MG) third and Abecassis fourth in his Alta. The regular sidecar race had preceded the final, and to round the day off there was another Palace 'first', a five-lap Ladies' Race, won by Mrs Lace in an Alta from Kay Petre's Riley and Mrs Thomas in a Delahaye.

In the relaxed atmosphere of these prewar race meetings, where the friendly rivalry of the mainly amateur competitors was in sharp contrast with the highly paid professionalism of the higher echelons of the sport today, amusing incidents abounded – attitudes to safety, too, were vastly different from those of more recent years! During one motorcycle event, a Norton-mounted competitor who shall be nameless got it all wrong approaching North Tower Crescent and went up the earth bank (no crash barriers in those days) weaving in and out of the trees at great speed until he finally hit one, neatly felling it and sending it crashing across the track. The unfortunate rider broke his false teeth in the incident, although he was otherwise unhurt and both he and the bike were able to compete again later in the day, but it required the combined efforts of six strong marshals to clear the fallen tree from the circuit. After practice at another meeting, one competitor failed to turn up in the paddock and could not be found stranded on the circuit with a broken-down machine. A sharp-eyed marshal eventually saw him and his Triumph lying side-by-side covered in mud at the bottom of a dried-up lake. He was fine when he'd been brought round, and the bike only needed a good clean!.

On balance, car racing was proving to be more popular than motorcycling, so the Road Racing Club, ever watchful of crowd figures, decided to drop the experiment of sidecar races at the car meetings and replace them with sports car racing instead, using a Le Mans start, with drivers sprinting across the track to their cars, for extra interest. Another novelty introduced at this time was a £5 Forecast Competition, in which spectators were invited to predict the first five places and the winner's speed in the main race of the day, putting their completed entry forms from the programme in a collecting box provided.

As the political situation in Europe worsened in 1938, bringing the ever increasing threat of war, attendance at sporting events seemed to be if anything on the increase, as people looked for distractions to help them forget their worries for a while – where better in London than Crystal Palace? August 13 saw the crowds arriving for the first sports car race at the circuit. The Distillers Company took a full-page advert in the programme, proudly announcing that 19 of the 21 entries in this race were using alcohol fuel.

Prince Birabongse, who raced under the name B Bira, and his entourage, including Shura Rham (wearing spectacles) and Prince Chula (in the cap) celebrate the Siamese Prince's victory in the 1937 Imperial Trophy race with his ERA. Right: A youthful Count 'Johnny' Lurani and Luigi Villoresi, both of whom drove 1½-litre Maseratis in the same event, sporting different lines in goggles.

A serious-looking Percy Maclure with Johnny Wakefield and Tony Rolt after they had finished second, third and first, respectively, in the Crystal Palace Cup race in August 1938.

The following year ERA driver Raymond Mays, later to earn fame as the 'father' of the BRM project, became the winner of the Crystal Palace Cup, which has just been presented to him by Lord Howe.

Alcohol or not, from the Le Mans start, Arthur Dobson won in his Riley, despite valiant efforts from George Abecassis (Alta). However, in the following single-seater event, 15 laps for the Crystal Palace Cup, Abecassis got his win, leading the ERAs of Rolt, Wakefield and Dobson across the line.

The Motor Cycle backed the Coronation Grand Prix, scheduled for September 10, and announced to its readers that they could gain half-price admission with a coupon printed in the journal, a bargain at 1s 6d including parking. Advertised as an international event, with £300 in prize money as well as *The Motor Cycle* Trophy on offer, it looked very promising. But by the end of August it became apparent to the club that although some top riders had entered, a clash of dates with the Manx Grand Prix and a Brooklands fixture meant that the entry list was just too small to make the meeting worthwhile and it was cancelled.

A very different motorcycle event had been held on the August Bank Holiday Monday when a motorized Medieval Tournament was held, with BBC television in attendance.

Amusements provided for the crowd included motorcycle-mounted knights and damsels playing darts, hoop-la and quintain, Wild West duellers, maypole rides, and chariots drawn by motorbikes on the speedway track.

The final event of the 1938 season was the second running of the Imperial Trophy, on October 8, and once again the BBC televised the event, with Alan Hess as commentator. Events in Munich cast a shadow over the meeting, but the Road Racing Club hoped that a good international entry list, the best yet seen at the Palace, plus the prospect of a special five-lap match race between arch-rivals Dobson and Bira, would entice the crowds to the circuit, even if the weather saw fit to dampen their enthusiasm somewhat. A silver cup for the winner and a silver casket for the runner-up were to be awarded for the match race, and for the main event there was ample prize money and the Imperial Trophy, as well as Road Racing Club awards and 'bannerettes', to ensure keen competition. Another trophy, presented by Hon Peter Beatty, owner of

The start of the 1939 Crystal Palace Cup race with George Abecassis' Alta (9) taking an initial lead from the ERAs of Raymond Mays (6) and Prince Bira (3), Percy Maclure's Riley (16) and the Hon Peter Aitken's ERA (15). Car 12 is Arthur Dobson's ERA.

the Derby winner Bois Roussel, was to be presented to the lap record holder at the end of each season.

At 2.30pm the meeting kicked off with the match race. Prince Bira and Arthur Dobson were joint lap record holders, driving similar 1½-litre ERAs, and they had already had several memorable tussles, so close competition was on the cards. They were indeed very evenly matched but the crowd groaned with disappointment when Romulus punctured a rear tyre on the third lap and Bira had to stop. In the main race, however, Bira was unstoppable in Heat 1, winning from Abecassis, Wakefield and Connell. Dobson took Heat 2 from the MG of Cuddon-Fletcher, Tony Rolt's ERA and the Scuderia Ambrosiana Maserati of Eugenio Minetti. Then, for the final, it rained heavily. Some of the principal competitors fitted twin rear wheels, as they did for hill climbing, and in these conditions the independent rear suspension of the Alta perhaps gave George Abecassis an advantage over the beam-axle ERAs, for he was just able to beat Bira, with Minetti third and Rolt fourth.

So the 1938 season at the Palace ended on a high note, and the Road Racing Club looked forward to the next season with confidence. By the time 1939 began, the rejuvenated speedway team was in full swing, and, much to the annoyance of many of the spectators who had supported the motorcycle events on the road circuit, the Road Racing Club announced its intention to drop all motorcycle races from the programme. Some felt that the two-wheelers had not been given fair treatment as the car races had invariably been allocated the best dates, bank holidays for example, but there had also been complaints about high admission costs, and the weather and a bus strike had all combined to keep the crowds at the bike meetings small. The cancellation of the previous year's Coronation Grand Prix had really decided the issue finally for the organizers. So the 1939 season was planned with only car races on the programme: in fact, of course, much more momentous happenings were soon to overtake everyone's plans in Europe. . .

Meanwhile, on April 15, 1939, the new season began with the eighth running of the Stanley Cup competition, previously run first at Brooklands and then in 1937 and 1938 at Donington Park, organized not by the Road Racing Club but jointly by the Frazer Nash and BMW Car Club and the Vintage Sports Car Club. Sir Arthur Stanley was patron of the event which consisted of team relay and handicap races for members of the competing clubs and a race for pre-1915 cars. The 'link' circuit was to be used for the first time for a car race. Competitors proceeded normally from the start but three-quarters of the way down Terrace Straight they would turn sharp right round Cedar Pond, rejoining the full circuit at Big Tree Bend and thus missing North Tower Crescent, The Glade, Fisherman's Bend, Fisherman's Rise and the Pond Hairpin. The length of this shorter circuit was 1.193 miles.

All the entrants were amateur clubmen, out for a good day's sport, and the cars ranged from the 747cc Austin Seven to a massive 21-litre Benz! In between was a wide selection including Bugatti, Bentley, Austro-Daimler, Amilcar, Wolseley, MG, Singer, Riley, and of course many Frazer Nashes and Frazer Nash BMWs. John Bolster was on the list with his famous sprint machine Bloody Mary, primly rendered 'Bolster Special' in the programme! Notable names among those entered for the Team Relay Handicap included Bob Gerard, driving a Riley for the United Hospitals and University of London Motor Club team, eventual winners of the race, and R R C (Rob) Walker, driving a Delahaye in the Cambridge University Automobile Club team. Walker was to become well known after the war as the entrant of a variety of racing cars driven by Stirling Moss among others.

The Road Racing Club were back in charge on May 20, and the BBC were back to televise the event, the Sydenham Trophy Meeting. It began on a light-hearted note with the semi-finals of the Boy Scout Soap Box Derby held on the section of track between New Zealand Scoreboard and the grandstands. Something like 150 pedal-powered racers, none of which according to the rules should have cost the scout troop who built it more than 50 shillings, were to take part – another 'first', the Road Racing Club proudly proclaimed. Scouts from all over the South East arrived and their mounts had names like 1066 Special (entered by the 3rd Hastings Troop), Caesar Romanus (1st Dunmow), Catfish (6th Weymouth Sea Scouts) and the 8th Croydon's Bitza Special No 8 (what happened to the other seven is not recorded). Great fun for all concerned!

Racing proper involved all the Palace favourites including Bira, Dobson, Abecassis, Rolt, Ruesch and Maclure. John Bolster returned, his car Bloody Mary still politely referred to as a 'Bolster' in the programme. Dobson took Heat 1, business as usual, but after a fierce struggle Bira had to settle for second in Heat 2 as Hans Ruesch in the Alfa Romeo got the better of the 'eight-stone of dynamite from Siam' as the programme called him. The final once again saw the two ERAs out in front, though Ruesch was never far behind. This time, Bira took the honours. Johnny Wakefield was a fairly distant fourth, also in an ERA. Bira rounded off a successful day by winning the Sydenham Plate race for sports cars in his Delahaye.

Even now, as war began to seem more and more inevitable, the Road Racing Club looked forward to their next event, though space in the programme was given over

to serious announcements like 'National Service – We MUST be Prepared'. Also in the programme was an appeal for the British Motor Racing Fund, to help ERA: Humphrey Cook, who had sunk something like £75,000 into the project, could go no further unaided and there were still those who cherished the hope that his team might be able to provide Britain with a competitive Grand Prix car. Hindsight tinges their 'press-on-regardless' optimism with almost painful irony to the postwar observer.

Adding to the gloom cast by the gathering war clouds over the Palace meeting on July 1 was the news that Richard Seaman had died from burns received when he crashed his Mercedes-Benz in the Belgian Grand Prix at Spa the previous week. Seaman had been a first class ambassador for British motor racing, and he was a keen supporter of Crystal Palace too: his death was a cruel blow to motor sport. A minute's silence was observed in his memory prior to the start of the Crystal Palace Cup race. There were a few non-starters among the Palace regulars, but Raymond Mays returned to the circuit with a 2-litre ERA, not having been seen there during the 1938 season. Heat 1 went to Bira, with Mays not far behind. Heat 2 saw Bert Hadley (Austin) win from Percy Maclure (Riley), and a troubled Arthur Dobson could manage only fifth. His brother, Bill Dobson, driving a

Raymond Mays out-braking George Abecassis as they contest the lead of the Crystal Palace Cup race at Stadium Dip.

Another day, another battle. A month later Mays was locked in close combat with Dobson, both their ERAs wearing twin rear tyres, which were a popular innovation at the time aimed at improving traction.

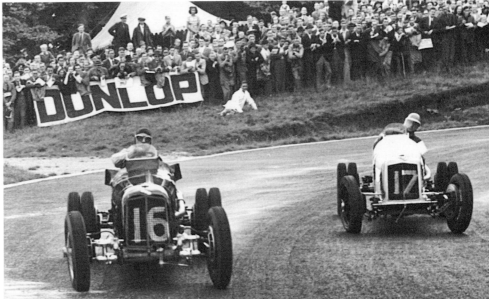

Riley, took the honours in the Crystal Palace Plate for sports cars, from Fane's Frazer Nash and Abecassis in an Alta. Then there was a Vintage Cup race won by Hampton's 1910 Bugatti before the final, run as usual over 16 laps. The two ERAs of Mays and Bira had a terrific three-cornered scrap with Hadley's little Austin. Mays set a scorching fastest lap at 1min 58.1sec (60.92mph), the first time the 2min/60mph barrier had been broken and a record on the 2-mile circuit which would stand for all time. Bira tried hard for second place but had to settle for third as Hadley crossed the line two-tenths of a second in front of him and some three seconds behind Mays.

'There is no doubt about it,' enthused the report in *The Motor*, 'racing at Crystal Palace gets better and better, and crowds, thrilled with a close-up view of the sport, get larger and larger. Racing was the finest yet on this excellent circuit which so closely resembles a typical Continental round-the-houses course – without the houses. . . I have never seen a crowd so excited.' *The Autocar* enjoyed the event too: 'Blue skies, big crowds, and records falling like skittles. Then came the final – and what a final!' *Light Car and Cyclecar* had the last word: 'A magnificent end to a wonderful afternoon.'

The Road Racing Club had decided to swap the Imperial Trophy race from its usual October date and run it in August, with the London Grand Prix reverting to the autumn fixture. So Saturday, August 26 saw the third running of the Imperial Trophy, just eight days, as it turned out, before the outbreak of World War 2. Despite the impending cataclysm hanging over the nation that day, the enthusiasts were determined more than ever to enjoy their motor sport, though none could have guessed that this was the last time that the Palace would be used for racing for 14 years. Bira's non-appearance for Heat 1 was a disappointment, and allowed Bert Hadley a fairly comfortable win in his Austin from Stuart-Wilton (MG). Heat 2 saw Raymond Mays win from Arthur Dobson. Abecassis took the sports car honours in his Alta and Hampton's Bugatti again won the Vintage Cup. The honour of what was to be the last win on the 2-mile circuit (though nobody knew it at the time) went to Hadley, coming home in the final nearly 2 minutes ahead of Dobson who set fastest lap, though unable to match Mays' record. The MGs of Stuart-Wilton and Nickols were third and fourth.

You could have won 10 shillings' worth of tickets for the October 7 meeting in a 'Speedyard Limerick' competition but alas that meeting, the London Grand Prix, was destined never to be held and many of the young men at the Palace, competitors, officials and spectators alike, were destined to be in khaki within a very short space of time as war engulfed Europe. Crystal Palace would eventually emerge from its wartime role ready for motor racing in a new and faster form, but all that was a long time in the future as Britain braced itself for the unknown in that late summer of 1939.

A rather more sedate pace around Crystal Palace. This is Bird's Enfield leading Rowe's single-cylinder Swift in a two-lap handicap race for cars built up to 1913 which formed part of the July 1939 meeting.

CHAPTER 5

Crystal Palace in a postwar guise

Racing on a shorter but faster track, 1953 to 1959

When hostilities finally ended in 1945, the park at Crystal Palace was in a state of decay. The Ministry of Defence slowly cleared their remaining tanks and guns from the site, and a few unexploded bombs had to be removed, too. The last remaining relics of the Palace itself, the North and South Towers, had gone, demolished during the early part of the Blitz because it was feared that they provided the Luftwaffe with a good landmark during raids on South London, which had suffered badly in the bombing.

Renovation began under the direction of the London County Council, now in charge of the site. By 1951, they had decided that the time was right for motor racing to reappear at the venue, and the Crystal Palace Motor Sports Committee was appointed to organize it for them. This body was made up of representatives from various car and motorcycle racing clubs and others connected with the promotion of motor sports. Many local residents, however, did not share this enthusiasm for the return of motor sport, not relishing the idea of their weekends being accompanied by the roar of racing machinery once again, and they were less submissive about it than in prewar years. They obtained a court injunction limiting the number of days for racing to five per year, and this limitation would run right through to the end of the 1960s.

In spite of this resistance, the Motor Sports Committee threw themselves energetically into reviving racing, and one of the first decisions was that the 2-mile track with its twisting inner loop was too slow, so the New Link, a fast 1-in-8 downhill section, was added, reducing the circuit length to 1.39 miles by joining Fisherman's Bend to the start/finish straight. In early May, 1953, the workmen finishing off the track alterations by erecting crash barriers paused to lean on their shovels and watch the first cars since before the war to use the Crystal Palace circuit for official practice and testing. The postwar Palace looked rather different with its shorter circuit, the towers gone, and the disappearance too of the last of the replica government buildings at South Tower Corner which had finally crumbled away.

On Whit Monday, May 23, 1953 (coincidentally, like 1937, Coronation Year), racing returned to Crystal Palace, now advertised as 'London's Own Circuit'. The British Automobile Racing Club organized the meeting for the London County Council by arrangement with the Crystal Palace Motor Sports Committee. A page in the programme was filled with greetings to the reborn circuit from drivers including some of the prewar Palace aces: Raymond Mays, George Abecassis, Prince Bira, Tony Rolt and Robin Hanson all wished the forthcoming events well, and newcomers Ken Wharton and the 23-year-old Stirling Moss expressed their eagerness to participate. The differences in the circuit would obviously change its character, making it significantly faster apart from anything else, a development which was generally welcomed. Competitors were also pleased to see a new and larger paddock, adjacent to the start/finish straight on the site of the old speedway oval, with access by the bridge across Ramp Bend.

This first event, billed as an International, attracted 42,438 paying spectators to the Palace, and the entry list for the main race, the Coronation Trophy for Formula 2 cars (at that time up to 2 litres unsupercharged or 500cc supercharged) included among others four Connaughts, the works cars of Roy Salvadori and John Coombs, Tony Rolt in Rob Walker's and another for Ken McAlpine, Lance Macklin and Peter Collins in HWMs, a Cooper-Alta for Stirling Moss, and Ken Wharton's Cooper-Bristol.

Heat 1 began the meeting at 2pm and was won by Tony Rolt, setting the first lap record for the revised circuit at 72.73mph. Ken Wharton, Lance Macklin and Stirling Moss followed him home to qualify for the final. Heat 2 saw a win for Peter Whitehead in his Cooper-Alta from Peter Collins (HWM). Graham Whitehead (Peter Whitehead's cousin) was third in a Cooper-Bristol with Jack Fairman's HWM fourth.

Before the final, the crowd were entertained by a 500cc Formula 3 race. Stirling Moss took the honours in his

Cooper, setting the new lap record for the formula at 70.68mph, ahead of Reg Bicknell (Erskine Staride), Stuart Lewis-Evans, George Wicken, Don Parker and Jimmy Brown (later of Silverstone circuit fame). The next race, for supercharged cars up to 1,500cc, provided an outing for some of the prewar racing machinery, and Graham Whitehead won in his ERA with updated bodywork. Tony Rolt was runner-up in a Delage.

Eleven cars lined up for the final of the Coronation Trophy Race, Ken Wharton (Cooper-Bristol) leading off the line to win from Tony Rolt's Connaught. Final event of the day was a sports car race, which rounded off a varied programme to the satisfaction of drivers and spectators alike. The new shorter circuit had proved successful and once more Crystal Palace was turning out to be an excellent venue: despite the opposition of some local residents, the future looked bright.

Motorcycle racing returned to the Palace on Saturday, June 27, 1953, and 9,018 spectators came through the gates to see it. Many of the riders who had raced there before the war returned, and there were some new faces, too. Maurice Cann was back, and other names entered included Bob Geeson, Ernie Barrett, Derek Powell, Bob Keeler, Pip Harris and Cyril Hale. Another entry, then just 19 years old, who was destined to make a big name for himself not only at the Palace but also much further afield, on two wheels and four, was John Surtees. John's father, John senior, known as Jack, was of course well known to Palace fans for his sidecar racing exploits at the circuit before the war, and he ran a motorcycle shop in nearby West Wickham. The family lived not far from Crystal Palace at Addington. Jack had retired from racing to help John in his career, and the young Surtees already had a string of wins behind him. He had recently returned from the Isle of Man TT races, where he had been offered a works Norton ride by Joe Craig, obviously impressed by his performance on his own Norton. Surtees had already agreed to ride Dr Joe Erlich's EMC in the Junior TT and could not let the owner down, but the

EMC proved to be his downfall, the forks breaking at the Ballaugh Bridge jump in practice, pitching him off and breaking his left wrist. Unable to compete, Surtees had left the island before race week began. John Surtees jnr (as the programme called him) had a far from happy first meeting at the Palace, retiring in one race and non-starting a second. Subsequent meetings proved more successful, and during the 1950s Surtees was rarely out of the record book at Crystal Palace, notching up 31 wins at the circuit, an unequalled feat. He went on to be the only man to win World Championships on both bikes and cars, and became a team manager building his own Formula 1 and 2 cars. Fittingly, one of his cars is credited in the records with the fastest-ever lap of the 1.39-mile circuit. In 1953, however, all that was in the future.

The organizing club, the British Motor Cycle Racing Club, or 'Bemsee', had hoped for a larger attendance that day, but the Wimbledon tennis finals were being held only a few miles away, as well as test cricket at Lords, and a date clash with the Dutch Grand Prix prevented factory teams from taking part. Prewar Palace star Maurice Cann, now Moto Guzzi mounted, won the first race of the day, Heat 1 of the 250cc event, the lap scorers miscounting and giving him the chequered flag a lap early! Bob Geeson (REG) took Heat 2. But it was the final that really brought the spectators to their feet: Ernie Barrett (Phoenix JAP) led from the line and was 250 yards in front after three laps. By half distance, Maurice Cann got his Moto Guzzi clear of the pack and set off in pursuit. Into the final lap, Cann still had about a hundred yards to make up but using all his Palace experience he began to achieve the seemingly impossible. He squeezed alongside Barrett on the last corner and the pair crossed the line almost as one, Cann getting the verdict by 0.2sec. One machine in this race, a Norton sleeved down to 250cc and ridden by B E Keys, had taken part in the very first Palace road racing meeting in May 1937, as a 350, ridden by Noel Pope.

Bob Keeler made it look very easy as he won his heat and

The North Tower on its way to the ground having been blown up in 1941 to remove a potential navigational aid from the unwelcome visitors from the Luftwaffe during World War 2.

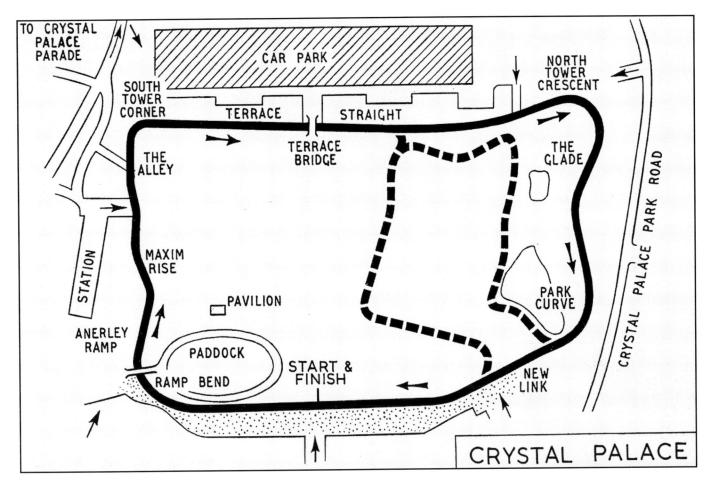

When the Crystal Palace circuit was reopened for racing in 1953 a new downhill link had joined the former Fisherman's Bend and Stadium Curve to eliminate the earlier inner loop and create a considerably faster 1.39-miles circuit.

Alan Brown's Cooper-Bristol receiving some attention in the Crystal Palace paddock prior to the sports car race at the first postwar meeting in May 1953.

A trio of HMW-Atlas ready to do battle for the first time on the Crystal Palace circuit. Although Stirling Moss was a regular member of the team, on this occasion he was driving his own Cooper-Alta and the most successful HWM drivers were Lance Macklin and Peter Collins.

Right, Tony Rolt, one of the most talented and stylish of British racing drivers of the early-postwar era, on his way to victory in the Crystal Palace Trophy race in July 1953 at the wheel of Rob Walker's Connaught.

Battling for the lead in the Coronation Trophy race, Ken Wharton and his Cooper-Bristol hold a temporary advantage over Lance Macklin's HWM and the Connaught of Tony Rolt, who went through to win.

Crystal Palace in May 1953 produced an interesting mix of prewar cars amongst the postwar machinery in the paddock, but although Graham Whitehead's ERA led all the way in the race for supercharged racing cars, Bill Goodwin only covered two laps before coasting to a halt in Kayley's car, seen here being warmed up.

the final of the 350cc event, then rounded off a successful day by winning the 500cc final. Heat 1 for sidecars saw a nasty accident befall the three-wheeler Morgan of Cyril Hale and his passenger Hadley: fortunately neither was seriously hurt but the Morgan was very badly damaged. E J Davis (Vincent) took the honours and Pip Harris won the second heat, these two joining battle in the final. Once again an error with the chequered flag resulted in confusion. This time, the marshal failed to put it out at the end of the 10-lap race, and on the unofficial eleventh lap Davis and Allen on their Vincent overtook the Norton of Harris and Mikos and were initially declared winners, but the officials subsequently realized their mistake and reinstated the Norton pair.

Before the next event at the Palace, the coronation of Queen Elizabeth II had ushered in a new Elizabethan age, so the Half-Litre Club, organizers of the July 11 meeting, rather patriotically put up a handsome Elizabethan Trophy for the winner of the 500cc Formula 3 race. With 60 entrants, the racing was split into four 10-lap heats and a final, but only a relatively small crowd of 7,823 spectators were there to see it. Harold Daniell, another local favourite with a motorcycle business in nearby Forest Hill, well known to bike racing fans for his prewar Palace exploits and his wins in the Isle of Man Senior TT in 1938, 1947 and 1948, had

entered an Emeryson-Norton, having retired from two-wheeler racing. Other names included Les Leston (Leston-Norton), Cliff Allison (Cooper-Norton) and Austin Nurse, who used to squeeze his 17-stone frame into the cockpit of a Cooper. Heat winners were Ivor Bueb (Arnott), Stuart Lewis-Evans (Cooper), Reg Bicknell (Erskine Staride) and Charles Headland (Martin). The final, the Elizabethan Trophy and £35 prize money went to Lewis-Evans from Leston, John Brown, Dennis Taylor and Ivor Bueb.

The large entry and diversity of marques bore witness to the vigorous growth of the 500c movement which was to prove such a valuable training-ground for postwar motor sport in this country. It is interesting to note that every car and engine used during this meeting was from a British manufacturer.

In the other trophy race of the day, the Crystal Trophy, a cut-glass sherry barrel, plus another £35, was won by Tony Rolt in Rob Walker's Connaught, with Roy Salvadori second in a similar car. A couple of consolation F3 races were held to round off the meeting, Harold Daniell taking the 'Petit Prix', adding a four-wheeled win to his bike successes, and Les Leston winning the half-litre invitation race.

The Auto-Cycle Union was celebrating its Golden Jubilee in 1953, and the meeting organized by them on

August 22 was expected to attract a good entry and large crowds. Unfortunately, the day was marred by bad weather, and the threat of heavy rain, although it did not actually materialize, in addition to the withdrawal of some top names, was enough to keep attendance down so that only 6,392 paying customers were recorded. Among the absentees from the entry list were Maurice Cann and Bob Keeler, the latter still unfit after a nasty fall at Oliver's Mount in July. Then, during practice, John Surtees made a rare mistake, injured his elbow and had to withdraw from the rest of the proceedings.

With depleted grids, the racing was, like the weather, rather dull, although Mick O'Rourke livened up the 350cc final with a spirited chase from fourth place, first dicing with J R Clark (AJS) and G Monty (GMS), then overhauling the leader Percy Tait (Norton) to win, setting joint fastest lap with Tait in the process.

Pip Harris was eventually declared winner of the three-wheeler race. He misunderstood the flag marshal and stopped after nine laps when he had a massive lead. Although Bill Boddice (Norton) and J Beeton (Norton) went on to complete the tenth lap, both sportingly said that as they could never have caught Harris the result at the end of the ninth lap should stand.

The final of the 1,000cc race did produce a close finish. Percy Tait led for most of the distance, closely followed by R A Russel on his Norton, Mick O'Rourke and P E S Webb (JABS). On the last lap, Russel made his move and after dicing side-by-side with Tait crossed the line some 3ft ahead.

With road safety in mind, the RAC/ACU publicized their Motor Cycle Training Scheme at this meeting. It was announced that novice riders would shortly have the chance to learn motorcycle control in complete safety on the Crystal Palace Circuit. The proposed course of tuition would consist of 12 lectures and 12 lessons. The practical lessons would begin with various low-speed slalom tests laid out on the straight to enable the rider to get the feel of the machine. For the fee of £1 16s (about £1.80), the novice would get some nine hours in the saddle plus the attention of a team of 20 instructors. Similar schemes were tried in Gillingham and Guildford but with less success than at Crystal Palace mainly because those towns lacked suitable off-road training areas. The Palace circuit offered the ideal venue for young motorcyclists to get thoroughly used to their machines before venturing onto public roads.

The training had to stop on race days, though, and the next event, the last of the 1953 season, was on September 19 when the Half-Litre Club organized an International Race Meeting consisting of Formula 2 and 3 heats and a couple of sports car races. Attendance was up, with 13,244 people arriving to watch the action, and the programme was opened by Heat 1 of the RedeX Trophy for 500cc F3 cars. This was won by Don Parker's Kieft from Ivor Bueb and Johnny Brise in Arnotts, with Don Truman fourth. Next onto the circuit came a rather depleted field of seven F2 cars, five of the entry list, including Ken Wharton (Cooper-Bristol), Ron Flockhart (Connaught) and Paul Emery in his own Emeryson, non-starting for various reasons. Stirling Moss won from pole position in his Cooper-Alta at an

average speed of 70.68mph. Behind him came Tony Rolt (Connaught) and Bob Gerard (Cooper-Bristol). Bernie Ecclestone brought his Cooper-Bristol home sixth.

Events three and four were the other heats for the 500cc cars, and resulted in wins for Stuart Lewis-Evans from Moss, Wicken, Bicknell and Jim Russell (later famous for his racing drivers' school), and for Leston ahead of Brandon and Gerard. Once again only seven cars came to the grid for the second part of the Formula 2 race for the London Trophy, though Flockhart did manage to start in his Connaught this time and was to finish third. Stirling Moss repeated his first-heat win and Rolt was second.

Next came the Formula 3 final, with Stuart Lewis-Evans on pole and Stirling Moss, Don Parker and George Wicken beside him. Lewis-Evans was in winning form, his Cooper taking the chequered flag from Don Parker's Kieft. Moss seemed to be heading for a comfortable third place, but he overdid it and spun off with two laps to go, letting Wicken move up into third with Brandon and Gerard fourth and fifth.

The Norbury Trophy race was for sports cars over 1,500cc and saw Alan Brown in his Cooper-Bristol win from the Tojeiro-Bristol of Cliff Davis. Ian Burgess had driven a superb race from the back of the grid, after last-minute trouble with his Kieft-Bristol prevented him from taking his front-row position, and almost took second from Davis but the Tojeiro driver 'shut the door' on his opponent.

After a consolation race for the F3 cars, won by Jack Westcott in a Kieft, the Anerley Trophy race for the smaller sports cars saw Bob Said, an American driving an OSCA, win from Ian Burgess (Kieft). Another entrant in that race was Colin Chapman, described in the programme as a 'rather unusual young man' because he was both driving and building cars for the fledgling Team Lotus. No-one at the Palace that day could have guessed that the frail-looking Lotus with its 1,172cc side-valve engine would be the forerunner of all those innovative and successful Grand Prix cars which would follow over the next three decades.

The season had established that Crystal Palace was very definitely back in action after a gap of 14 years. The circuit had now begun its longest period of uninterrupted use, and 19 seasons were to pass before it fell silent once more. Motor sport now began to fall into a regular pattern at the Palace, with the London County Council letting various clubs run meetings on three bank holidays and a couple of Saturdays each year. It might seem like wasteful under-use of the excellent circuit and facilities which had been established, but the LCC had to strike a balance between pleasing motor sport enthusiasts and angering the local populace with the noise of unsilenced racing engines, a balance effectively enforced by the court injunction limiting the number of days' racing. Most seasons would now see two motorcycle race meetings and three for cars.

So the 1954 season began on Easter Monday, April 19, with a meeting organized by the ACU which had attracted no fewer than 210 entries. Practice sessions were held on the previous Saturday, and these drew a large crowd, many of the competitors coming from Brands Hatch were they had been racing on Good Friday. On Easter Monday a total of 24,475 paying spectators lined the terraces round the track, braving the cold wind but thankful that the clouds which threatened

Wheel-to-wheel through Ramp Bend. Paul Emery, driving his Formula 3 Emeryson in typically exuberant style, takes the wide line as he prepares to move up a place.

Stirling Moss, his Formula 3 Cooper-Norton immaculately turned out and, as usual, carrying the racing number 7, prepares for the RedeX Challenge Trophy final in September 1953, but a deflated tyre would put him out of the race. John Cooper is fastening the engine cover behind him.

rain all the morning had cleared in time for the first race at 1.30pm. This was for 200cc machines, a category which did not receive much support from British manufacturers, so the crowd were treated to the then novel sight of Continental racing bikes dominating the race. There were some over-bored BSAs and the like taking part, but among the front-runners a two-man contest developed between John Hogan on an MV Agusta and Maurice Cann on an FB Mondial. After a terrible start, leaving the grid last but one, Cann rode superbly through the field to catch Hogan on the final lap but just failed to beat the MV rider across the line.

Next out were the competitors in Heat 1 of the 250cc race. In this class, once again, few British companies produced any real racing machines, so many riders either had to make do with prewar Rudges or modified road bikes. The fast boys, however, had Italian bikes or specials, and John Surtees was entered to ride one of the most interesting of the latter. The REG was a 250cc double-overhead-camshaft parallel twin built close to Crystal Palace, in Croydon, at the home of Bob Geeson. Geeson himself had raced the machine and done well enough to show how good it might be in the hands of a top-class rider. Surtees had already ridden it well at Brands Hatch on Good Friday, and at the Palace in front of a big crowd enjoying glorious spring

weather he won his heat and the final, setting a new 250cc lap record at 69.31mph and a new race record, in spite of the efforts of E W Tinkler on a Pike-Rudge, who led initially, and Maurice Cann on his Moto Guzzi, the winner of the second heat, who chased him across the line.

Much of the sport showed little or no sign at this period of the impact of the professionalism that was to come – enthusiasm abounded, and riders raced purely for the fun of it. H D German, for example, rode a modified 1935 Sports Rudge in the 250 race, a 350cc Keele Norton, a 500cc JV Special, and was also passenger on B Denton's Coventry Eagle sidecar outfit. In all he was down to cover some 90 racing miles that afternoon! W J Jenness was in his late fifties and at a time when many men are looking forward to a quiet retirement he was still racing his Velocette, continuing a career on two wheels that he had begun as a dispatch-rider in the First World War and had continued at Brooklands and Donington as well as in 17 appearances on the Isle of Man. Many other riders, with no hope of outright victory, proudly wheeled out much-modified road machines, the product of many hours spent in garages and sheds burning the midnight oil and attempting to extract just a little more speed than their rivals.

By contrast, the 350cc race consisted almost entirely of

The paddock area during one of the early postwar meetings. The purpose-built Rootes Group transporter was one of the most impressive motor racing vehicles of its time, but SU and KLG servicing was carried on out of a converted Bedford bus.

Stirling Moss in characteristic straight-arm pose at the wheel of his Cooper-Alta on his way to victory in his heat of the 1953 London Trophy race. Note the angle of drift he is holding through the right-handed bend.

The quiet before the storm. A grid full of 500cc Formula 3 cars and drivers in the paddock assembly area awaiting their turn on to the track. The staccato exhaust note from the single-cylinder engines would soon shatter the silence.

Jack Westcott and his Kieft-Norton holding a clear lead over Alec Cowley's Cooper-JAP and the rest of the field as they exit Ramp Bend on the first lap of their Formula 3 race during the September 1953 meeting.

British-built racing machines like the famous AJS 7R and the Norton 'Double Knocker', that term for the twin-overhead-camshaft engine being attributed to Harold Willis of Velocette. This race had international riders, too; Bob Cooper, the Canadian National Champion, who was gaining experience of British tracks before making his TT debut, and New Zealander Gavin Dunlop, an employee of Arter Bros who also entered him, both these men being AJS-mounted.

Four heats were needed to select the finalists for the 350cc race, and the winners were Ernie Washer (AJS), John Surtees (Norton), B Rood and J A Storr. The first heat was marred by a nasty accident when L Hall (BSA Gold Star) skidded while avoiding a bike on the ground. Out of control, he hit a group of photographers and received fatal injuries. One of the press men photographed the incident just before the unfortunate rider collided with him, the resulting picture being splashed sensationally across the tabloid papers the next day.

In the sidecar event, C Smith used his Norton to good effect to win his heat and the final. Then came the solo finals, providing good sport for the spectators with John Surtees dominating the 250, 350 and 1,000cc races, despite the valiant efforts of Maurice Cann in the 250 and J A Storr in the larger categories. Surtees also set new lap records for

the 250 and 350 classes and so could be well satisfied with his day's racing, though in the last race on the programme, an invitation event for the fastest 12 riders of the day, victory went to R H King (Norton).

On Whit Monday, 1954, two-wheelers of a different kind took to the circuit when the Palace hosted a Cycling Festival, featuring the finish of the Folkestone-London International Road Race. There were supporting races, events for children, and even a game of bicycle polo.

The next motorized event came on Saturday, June 18, when the BARC were in charge for a national car race meeting. Two heats for the Crystal Palace Trophy began the afternoon. Reg Parnell won the first from pole-position man Peter Collins who made a poor start in his Connaught, and Les Leston drove magnificently to take third in his 1,100cc Cooper-JAP. Parnell's Ferrari set a new lap record. R Nuckey took the second heat in a Cooper-Bristol.

Two races for 500cc cars followed, the first including the Crystal Palace debut of another name of note, Ken Tyrrell. The winner was Reg Bicknell in his home-built Revis which featured a futuristic full-width nose cone streamlined to help top speed. J K Hall in the Border Reivers Cooper took the second 500cc race.

The Club Trophy race saw Les Leston in his nimble

In August 1954 a lounge-suited Mike Hawthorn was invited to take a lap or two in the 2½-litre Ferrari with which Reg Parnell won the main event of the meeting.

Large-capacity sports cars took to the Crystal Palace track at the same meeting. Here, the Jaguar C-Type of Michael Head, whose son Patrick would earn fame as the designer of World Championship-winning Williams Formula 1 cars, leads the Aston Martin DB3 of Jocelyn Stevens at the approach to Ramp Bend. Note that the prewar grandstands have disappeared from the start-finish straight.

Right, a dramatic shot of P Overall and his passenger W James working hard to maintain the balance of their combination through a left-handed curve during the Easter Monday motorcycle meeting in 1955.

Cooper-JAP beat all the bigger cars round the twists and turns of the Palace circuit. Although dwarfed by the pursuing pack of Connaughts, front-engined Coopers and even prewar ERAs, the handling of the car and Leston's skill gave him the victory. Roy Salvadori in a Maserati led the sports car race for the first lap before Colin Chapman put his Lotus ahead. But Chapman retired on lap 4 leaving the Maserati to win from Alan Brown's Cooper and Tony Brooks in a Frazer Nash. The final of the Crystal Palace Trophy was the last race of the day; once again the Ferrari of Reg Parnell proved unbeatable and Peter Collins finished second in his Connaught. Around 13,000 people had spent another entertaining day at the races, again proving what an asset Crystal Palace was to London's sporting scene.

The circuit should have been bathed in summer sunshine for the 'Bemsee' meeting on July 17, but the rain gods saw fit to soak the track and the small crowd of around 3,000 people who braved the elements. With the raceway awash, speeds were kept down and many riders fell on the slippery surface, fortunately without serious injury. Despite the rain, John Surtees demonstrated his skill and his mastery of his local circuit – his dominance in the 250 race on the REG was such that he was arriving at Ramp Bend on the first lap while some of the riders were still push-starting on the grid.

Maurice Cann won the 125cc race on the FB Mondial, helped no doubt by the non-appearance of John Hogan's MV, but the popular Cann took a tumble in his 250cc heat and bent the wheel of his Moto Guzzi. Surtees ran away from the field in the 350cc race, but in the 1,000cc event he stopped with water in the carburettors after only two laps, when he already had a 10-second lead, leaving J R Clark (Matchless) to win from Mick O'Rourke. Pip Harris and Bill Boddice won their respective heats for the sidecar race, and a close battle developed between them in the final. However, Harris clipped a straw bale, tipping out his passenger who injured an arm, leaving Boddice to win. The wet crowd left the circuit impressed above all with the skill of John Surtees who was clearly a man to watch and possessed of a great deal of motorcycle racing skill.

August Bank Holiday brought sunshine and nearly 32,000 people to the palace to watch the BARC meeting. Once again Reg Parnell in his Ferrari provided the excitement as he took victory in the main race of the day from Roy Salvadori in a Maserati. Although the weather was good there were a number of crashes during the day. J K Hall shunted his Cooper-Bristol while dicing with Paul Emery (Emeryson-Alta), fortunately without serious injury, and in the sports car race, P R Crabb had the misfortune to suffer steering failure, the consequent lurid spin and crash at North Tower resulting in a very bent Kieft-Bristol, its split fuel tank leaving a very slippery and dangerous puddle on the racing line.

To end the 1954 season, the Half-Litre Club were back on September 18 with the RedeX Trophy for 500cc cars. Three heats were needed to sort out the finalists, Ivor Bueb taking Heat 1 from Reg Bicknell, Jim Russell winning Heat 2, and Les Leston Heat 3 from Ken Tyrrell. In the final, Ivor Bueb won the RedeX Trophy and £40 in his Cooper, ahead of Bicknell (Revis), Stuart Lewis-Evans (Cooper), Cliff Allison (Cooper), Don Parker (Kieft) and Les Leston also in a Cooper. The London Trophy race for Formule Libre cars was in two halves but both produced the same first three placings, Bob Gerard winning in his Cooper-Bristol from Don Beauman (Connaught) and Alan Brown (Cooper-Bristol). The Anerley Trophy sports car race went to Colin Chapman's Lotus from Archie Scott-Brown's Lister-MG, the Norbury Trophy to Tony Crook's Cooper, and the day was completed by a race for cars with JAP 500cc engines, Chris Lund winning from Henry Taylor and Tony Marsh, all in Coopers.

So another meeting was over, another season closed, and Crystal Palace went into its usual winter hibernation period until the familiar pattern began all over again on Easter Monday. That day, April 11, 1955, brought spring sunshine beaming down on the Palace, and a record crowd for motorcycle racing, 29,795 people, flocked through the gates. There was more competition among circuits than in earlier days, and some riders had gone to other meetings at Thruxton, Oulton Park and Cadwell Park, but nevertheless there was some fine racing and the by now usual brilliant display by John Surtees. In the 200cc race which opened the proceedings, the MV Agustas of J Baughn and A Hogan took the first two places. The first 350cc heat was comfortably won by Surtees (Norton), Frank Perris (AJS) took Heat 2 and Mick O'Rourke Heat 3. The final proved to be a race for second place as no-one could touch Surtees for overall victory. Behind the Norton rider, five AJS-mounted riders, Perris, O'Rourke, J P Ager, R Alderslade and Ernie Washer, struggled for the placings. After two laps they settled into a very close pack but stayed in unchanged order to the finish – O'Rourke, Perris and Washer, second third and fourth.

By comparison, the 250cc race was dull, with the field well spread out behind the almost inevitable winner, John Surtees (NSU Sportmax) from G H Turner (Rudge) and Percy Tait (Velocette). Surtees had also set two new lap records by this stage in the meeting. Next came the 1,000cc

event, and Heat 1 went to Mick O'Rourke (Norton), whose record of success at the Palace was overshadowed only by Surtees. Behind him there was a fantastic dice between Percy Tait (Triumph) and Eddie Grant, the South African champion who was having his first race in Britain. He quickly learned the tricky London circuit and shadowed Tait, never more than a few feet behind in third place. As Tait crossed the line he was amazed to see Grant alongside, and so were the timekeepers who could not split the pair and declared a dead heat for second place. Surtees was once more dominant in his heat and in the final where Grant made a poor start and Frank Perris took second place on his Matchless, Rutherford third and Tait fourth. The sidecar events proved rather dull and there was no effective competition for Bill Boddice who won his heat and the final in convincing form.

The meeting ended with a solo handicap race for the fastest dozen riders which produced a fine demonstration from Surtees who not only trounced the opposition but also equalled Reg Parnell's outright lap record, his 1,000cc Norton matching the Grand Prix Ferrari's average of 75.82mph round the Palace circuit.

By 1955, the Half-Litre Club, originally the 500 Club, had grown into the British Racing and Sports Car Club, and they were in charge of the Whit Monday meeting on May 30. More than 90 entries were attracted to the Palace as well as over 32,000 spectators. The main event was the London Trophy for Formula 1 cars, run as before in two 12-lap heats, with the aggregate of both to decide the winner. Everyone expected a repeat of the duel between Peter Collins and Roy Salvadori, both in 250F Maseratis, which had taken place three weeks earlier in the International Trophy race at Silverstone. Collins had won on that occasion, perhaps because his car had alloy wheels and disc brakes while Salvadori's retained the standard wire wheels and drum brakes. The first part of the Palace race did indeed see the two Maseratis first and second, Collins leading all the way but Salvadori having to dispose of Bob Gerard's Cooper-Bristol on the third lap. Part 2 initially looked like a re-run, but after two laps Salvadori's Gilby Engineering car stopped, leaving Peter Collins to take an easy win from Bob Gerard. (Gerard, incidentally, had announced his retirement at the end of the previous season, but that hadn't lasted long!)

Despite the name change, the BRSCC still promoted races for the 500cc F3 cars and the cars were still popular with drivers and spectators alike. The Whit Monday meeting again included the RedeX Trophy, with three heats to accommodate all the entries. The fastest F3 Coopers now had Norton power, replacing the ageing JAP engine, and Cooper-Nortons won all three heats in the hands of Ivor Bueb, Dennis Taylor and Cliff Allison. The final had commentator John Bolster describing a thrilling dice with Allison initially leading from Don Parker (Kieft), George Wicken (Cooper) and Ivor Bueb. On lap 3 Bueb began to challenge, passing Allison at half distance to take a lead he was not to lose, Wicken finishing second, Allison demoted to third on lap 9, and Parker fourth. The 'Petit Prix' consolation race for the F3s was won by Ian Raby (Cooper).

Sports car races completed the day's events, Ivor Bueb

and Les Leston enjoying a spirited scrap in the Anerley Trophy race (not Annerley with two Ns as in the programme!), victory going to Bueb with Austin Nurse third in his Lotus. The Norbury Trophy saw Salvadori looking determined to win in the one-off front-engined Cooper-Maserati built for Gilby Engineering, but he was overtaken by Archie Scott-Brown (Lister-Bristol) on lap 6.

Less than a fortnight later, motor sport made world headlines in the worst possible way with the tragedy at Le Mans in which 83 spectators were killed when a competing car scythed into the crowd. Repercussions included the banning of motor racing in Switzerland, Spain, Mexico and France, and while three of those countries later lifted the ban it remains in force to this day in Switzerland. Understandably, there was some anti-motor racing feeling in Britain too. Most people concerned, though, felt that it was a sport from which the element of risk could never be entirely eliminated, a fact recognized and accepted by both competitors and spectators. So there was no ban in this country. But what can be dated from June 1955 is an increasing concern with safety in motor sport, reflected in the gradual development of safety-conscious regulations over the ensuing years. The Crystal Palace circuit, with its relatively tight physical confines, was less well placed than many to take account of this evolution in attitudes, and while that was by no means the only factor in its eventual closure, it has realistically to be seen as one important reason why there is no longer motor racing in South East London.

Meanwhile, though, it was business as usual, and on June 18 'Bemsee' organized their meeting in fine style, blessed with fine weather. John Surtees was in his usual invincible Palace form, netting six wins from six starts. In the 250cc final he had a 17-second lead after only four laps! He had won his 250 heat, of course, and took heat and final wins in the 350 and Senior events. At the start of the second sidecar heat, Bruce Main-Smith got a real flyer – and left his partner Graves sprawling on the grid. The passengerless outfit was fine till it arrived at Maxim Rise where, lacking the necessary ballast, Main-Smith crashed out of the race. Bill Boddice won that heat and went on to take the final.

Such was the popularity of Crystal Palace as a racing venue that new spectator stands were erected before the next meeting, organized by the British Automobile Racing Club on July 30, 1955. 15,000 people arrived to fill them and see Mike Hawthorn make his Palace debut driving the silver-grey Maserati owned by Stirling Moss. The young Briton soon showed his world-champion potential when he took the first heat from the acknowledged Palace expert Roy Salvadori. Harry Schell was the winner of Heat 2 with his Vanwall. In the final it was Hawthorn from flag to flag, with Horace Gould, Harry Schell and Roy Salvadori scrapping behind him. By lap 2 Salvadori was in second place, with Gould gamely hanging on until lap 10 when he retired with transmission trouble. Hawthorn capped his success with a lap record at 78.93mph. The supporting 500cc race was a nail-biting affair with Jim Russell and Ivor Bueb dicing wheel-to-wheel. They crossed the line together, Russell just getting the decision. Reg Bicknell had a dramatic escape at Ramp Bend when his Revis-Norton lost a wheel. The meeting concluded a somewhat brief 1955 season at Crystal

A mixed field. Tony Crook's Cooper-Bristol sports car leading three single-seaters – Les Leston's Cooper-JAP, Mike Keen's Cooper-Alta and John Riseley-Prichard's Connaught – under the bridge at Ramp Bend in September 1954.

A driver's-eye view out of Park Curve and into the downhill New Link leading towards the start-finish straight. The car in the foreground is Dick Steed's Lotus-Climax Mark 8.

Mike Hawthorn in action again, this time at the wheel of the Maserati 250F with which he won the International Trophy race at the BARC meeting in 1955, followed home by Harry Schell's Vanwall and Roy Salvadori's Maserati.

Palace, a year rather overshadowed by events elsewhere in motor sport from which lessons would have to be learned.

When the early spring sunshine returned to the Palace on Easter Monday, April 12, 1956, so did John Surtees, bringing with him the beautiful 500cc four-cylinder MV Agusta, making its British debut in front of 26,000 racegoers. Surtees also had a 250cc MV, and Mick O'Rourke and Derek Minter were MV-mounted, too, though their engines were of a rather odd 203cc capacity, arrived at by using an over-bored 175cc unit. These bikes had proved very successful in the previous season when the works team had won many of the European races. They represented the state of the art in 1956 and were capable of beating many British machines of much larger capacity. Not surprisingly, it was John Surtees who won the 250cc event, setting a new class lap record at 72.10mph. J R Clark took the 350 race on his AJS. Surtees came within a whisker of the 1,000cc lap record as the four-cylinder MV took the Senior class, with J R Clark a close second. The day was rounded off by a handicap race for the fastest 20 riders, with John Surtees starting from scratch. He used the power and acceleration of the MV to great effect to pass many of the field, but the handicappers had his measure and he finished sixth: winner was the Norton of A V Hegbourne.

Cars filled the Whit Monday meeting on May 21, 1956, the BRSCC attracting an excellent entry and a crowd of over 35,000. The regular pattern of races for 500cc cars and sports cars supported the two-part London Trophy race. The first half saw a spirited dice between the Maserati of Stirling Moss and the rapid Alta-powered Emeryson of Paul Emery. Moss led off the line from pole position but on the second lap Emery took the lead. The two swapped places several times, and the Emeryson was ahead on lap 9. But when the all-important last lap finished it was Moss who took the flag. Throughout all the excitement, Bob Gerard held third place in his Cooper-Bristol. The result was the same in the second part, Moss again leading Emery across the line to win overall on aggregate and set a new lap record at 79.94mph. Emery was second and George Wicken third in a Cooper-Alta. Ivor Bueb in his Ecurie Demilitre Cooper-Norton won his F3 heat and went on to win the final, with the other heat winners Stuart Lewis-Evans and George Wicken second and third. Les Leston and Stirling Moss duelled in both sports car races and took a win each in their respective Cooper-Climax cars. The little bob-tail, centre-seat Coopers were very quick with only 1,500cc of Climax power, and featured the mid-engined layout which was as yet a novelty for sports-racing cars but would become universal in due course.

The BARC were in charge for the August Bank Holiday car races on August 6, 1956, and though it was wet for the morning practice session, they were blessed with a dry afternoon. Despite the uncertain weather, 10,000 people turned up and were treated to a thrilling first heat for the

Stirling Moss had a busy and successful day at the BRSCC meeting at the 'Palace' in May 1956 when he and his Maserati 250F won both parts of the London Trophy race for Formule Libre cars, with Paul Emery and his Emeryson, seen here in the background, finishing runner-up. Moss also climbed aboard the centre-seater Cooper-Climax and won the Norbury Trophy sports car race.

F L Fuller leading R J Haydon and A W Kimber amongst a group of 10 riders streaming into Ramp Bend during the 250cc solo race at the 1955 Easter Monday meeting. Note the closely packed terraces on this sunny Bank Holiday afternoon.

August Trophy sports car race. Cliff Allison (Lotus 11) led from the start but from the back of the grid the Lotus of Keith Hall carved through the field to be on Allison's tail by the second lap. On lap 8 Hall got by and went on to win a close race. Heat 2 was dull by comparison, with W Ellis winning from M Zervudachi, both in Lotus 11s. The final produced another fierce scrap between Hall and Allison, the former winning by a second. The ultra-light Lotus had eclipsed the Cooper in the small-capacity sports car class because of its greater sophistication in chassis design, though Lotus designer Colin Chapman stuck to front engines at this stage.

Bikes were back for the final meeting of the 1956 season, with a rather late date of October 6. Some riders found that falling leaves at these autumn meetings made the track very slippery, particularly through The Glade, the wooded area of the circuit. 'Bemsee' had received over 150 entries for the meeting, including two riders making the trip all the way from Scotland, because it was their final meeting of the season and many of the BMCRC championships were still to be decided that afternoon.

Although the day was sunny, a cool autumn wind kept the crowd down to below 5,000. Nevertheless, the action on the track warmed the enthusiasts on the terraces. With a crowded programme, proceedings commenced at 11.30am with Heat 1 of the 350cc race. The main contenders were John Hartle (Norton), Bob Anderson (AJS) and Bob

McIntyre, also on a Norton, who was leading the championship, and it was McIntyre who scored the first of his wins that day, though Bob Anderson raised the lap record to 72.52mph. Heat 2 went to Alastair King (Norton), and the crowd were disappointed when Cecil Sandford non-started on his three-cylinder DKW. The 500cc heats followed the lunch break, with McIntyre (Norton) a winner again in the first and John Clark (Matchless) taking the second. Next were two sidecar heats, won by Pip Harris and A Young. Another entrant in the sidecar class, Owen Greenwood, had a passenger, according to the programme, by the name of 'E Quillibrium'! Then there was a race within a race as the 125cc entry was boosted by seven 50cc racers, amongst them Miss P M Dale on a Britax (though she was unable to start) and Frank Sheene, father of Barry, on his Astor Special, who took the honours in this class from G Peden whose mount was a modified NSU Quickly. Cecil Sandford won the 125cc race overall on an FB Mondial, setting a new lap record at 67.26mph to beat Mick O'Rourke's previous best of 66.72mph. Derek Edlin and John Baughn scrapped for second place, their similar MV Agusta machines rarely more than a few feet apart, the verdict going to Edlin. Next came the 250cc final, where Bob McIntyre lapped everybody except the second and third men who were Geoff Monty on his GMS and R M Harding on a GMV which was another Monty-built machine. Arthur Wheeler had swapped his Guzzi for a ride

The master at work. No-one stamped his authority on the demanding Crystal Palace circuit more emphatically than John Surtees. Although he was Norton's team leader at the time, he rode in a private capacity at the 1955 Easter Monday meeting, using his own Norton machine. As usual, he dominated the day, during which he set a new record lap at 75.82mph, equalling the fastest previously recorded at the track by Reg Parnell in a Ferrari.

Right, Surtees had switched to the Italian MV Agusta team by the time he returned to Crystal Palace one year later, bringing with him both 500cc and 250cc machines, the former's four-cylinder engine bringing an exciting new high-pitched sound to South East London.

on the latest REG from Bob Geeson and brought the machine home to an excellent fourth. In contrast McIntyre had to work hard to win the 350cc race as Terry Shepherd hounded him, breaking Bob Anderson's short-lived lap record in the process, leaving it at 76.28mph. When Shepherd dropped back a little he too was hounded by Alan Trow who passed him several times. All three riders were on Nortons and the ding-dong battle had the crowd on their feet. The pace slowed a little for the sidecar final in which Pip Harris scored an easy win, then quickened again as McIntyre, Trow and Anderson contested the Senior final and Shepherd made a supreme effort, his Norton coming from the back of the field to third place before falling back with a misfire to finish eleventh. But the day belonged to Bob McIntyre. His triple win assured him of a triple championship title with the 250, 350 and 500cc BMCRC titles going his way. He had just signed a Gilera contract for the 1957 Grand Prix season, but announced that he would continue to work for Joe Potts as a mechanic in his Glasgow premises and ride his Nortons in British races.

If the last meeting of 1956 had seen a small crowd at the Palace, the 1957 season opener, the usual ACU meeting on Easter Monday, April 22, saw over 17,000 eager London race fans coming through the gates, despite the absence of many top names, away racing at Oulton Park, and a morning practice session once again dampened by showers. Many racing bikes were now sporting the full 'dustbin'

fairings which had a brief vogue before changing regulations outlawed them, though on the short straights at the Palace the aerodynamic advantage conferred on these streamlined machines was very slight. Indeed, on this occasion the best race of the day began with Peter Ferbrache (350 Norton) heading for a seemingly easy win on a machine uncluttered by any fairing. However, the similarly naked Norton of Bob Anderson was reeling him in, passing on the way both G C A Murphy (AJS) and Ned Minihan (Norton). On the eighth lap Anderson came out of Ferbrache's wheel tracks to grab the lead which he could just hold on to though unable to pull away, the close finish bringing the crowd to their feet. Anderson won again in the 500cc final, though he had a much easier time, winning by a 50-yard margin. In his heat he had settled for second place behind the Norton of G Tanner. Mick O'Rourke took both the 200cc and 250cc races though interest in the former had been focussed on second-place man S Rees on his MV Agusta because he showed undoubted skill at only 17 years of age. Geoff Monty held the lead for four laps in the 250cc race, his BSA-powered GMS leading the streamlined MV of O'Rourke, but then the positions were reversed and the Italian bike drew away to record a fairly easy win.

With another 'Bemsee' meeting next on the fixture list, on May 18, 1957, racegoers at the Palace were having a feast of motorcycle races. This time, however, it was club day and very few 'big names' were present, which perhaps explains the low turn-out with under 3,000 paying spectators. It was well organized, though: somebody said about the way 'Bemsee' ran the meeting, 'You could set your watch by the race starts'. Peter Ferbrache won both the 350 and 500cc finals. He enjoyed a spirited dice with Frank Perris in the smaller class, but Perris was a disappointed non-starter in the 500cc final because his Norton was inadvertently started with a piece of rag over the carburettor intake, put there because of an earlier rain shower, and this was sucked into the carb. Ferbrache was a very experienced all-rounder, having ridden in grass-track and speedway, and his road-racing performance at the Palace impressed many. Bill Boddice took a customary sidecar win and variety was added with 125 and 250cc races both going to Derek Edlin and a 50cc event won by C V Dawson (Itom). Spills were plenty in the wet and slippery conditions but only one rider needed a hospital check-up.

Four-wheeled racing returned on Whit Monday, June 10, when the BRSCC were in charge of a meeting with Formula 2 as the main attraction supported by Formula 3 and various classes of sports car. On a windy but warm and sunny day, the meeting was well supported by spectators and competitors alike. The Formula 2 field consisted entirely of Coventry Climax-powered cars: up against no less than 11

Coopers were just three Lotuses, the two works entries for Cliff Allison and Hugh Mackay-Fraser, and young Graham Hill driving Tommy Atkins' private entry. The Lotus was as yet a relatively unsorted design, but Cooper were riding the crest of a wave with their racers in most categories, and out of nine races at this Palace meeting a Cooper of one sort or another won five.

The main race, in two parts, the London Trophy for Formula 2 cars, produced a terrific dice between the two works Coopers of Palace favourite Roy Salvadori and an up-and-coming driver from Australia, Jack Brabham. The first half saw Salvadori leading from the start, but Brabham, once he had disposed of Mackay-Fraser's Lotus, stuck behind his team-mate like glue. George Wicken and Les Leston, both also in Coopers, were third and fourth. The Australian finished first in Part 2, breaking the lap record and clearly demonstrating to the crowd his great potential, and won the London Trophy on aggregate, followed by Wicken, Salvadori and Leston.

The RedeX Trophy for 500cc Formula 3 cars ran to four heats and a final. Heat winner Stuart Lewis-Evans took the final from Jim Russell, Don Parker, Tommy Bridger, Trevor Taylor and David Boshier-Jones, all six being Cooper-Norton drivers, such was the domination of the marque in

A smiling John Clark astride his 500cc Moto Guzzi in the Crystal Palace paddock assembly area during the April 1957 meeting. Despite what he was holding in his right hand, his streamliner was not being held together by string!

Crystal Palace attracted the very top people on both two and four wheels. Here is Mike Hailwood, a regular 'Palace' competitor, at the rain-soaked October 1958 meeting, during the course of which he won the 350cc race on this Norton as well as the 1,000cc event, having also won the 125cc race on a Ducati and the 250cc race on his FB Mondial. It was quite a day for 'Mike the Bike'!

this formula. Lotus had their revenge over Cooper in the sports car races, Colin Chapman beating Salvadori's Cooper to take the Norbury Trophy from Archie Scott-Brown's Elva, while Keith Hall in another works car led home his boss Chapman to take the Anerley Trophy, with Ian Raby third in the works Cooper. The only races not won by Cooper or Lotus that day were the Series Production sports car race which went to the AC Bristol of R D Jennings and the Unlimited sports car race won by the Lister-Jaguar of Archie Scott-Brown. A Cooper or Lotus chassis and Coventry Climax power – that seemed to be the winning combination, one that would go on eventually to establish Britain firmly in the forefront of Grand Prix racing.

By mid-season 1957, the 'new' shorter Crystal Palace circuit was five years old. At the BARC meeting on August 5, the drivers were asked for their comments on the revised circuit. Archie Scott-Brown said, '. . . the Palace is very fair in my estimation, because I have won several races there and so far I am glad to say I have not bent the car. The atmosphere and amenities are important. Here the Crystal Palace circuit ranks high. It is central, the meetings are friendly, the organizers helpful, and the amenities are more than adequate. Lastly, and by far the most important of all, is the circuit itself. The Palace is small but it is made up of practically every sort of corner, with two quite reasonable 120mph straights. It has up and downhill gradients, which make it more interesting than a flat aerodrome circuit. It also tests the driver because it is narrow with no room for mistakes. One must therefore drive on the limit but never exceed it or else a bent motor car is the least one can expect. Some people say it favours smaller cars, this is perhaps true to a certain extent, but any circuit can be a big-car circuit – I say this because I drive a big car.' The talented and enthusiastic Scott-Brown is of course best remembered for his stirring drives in the big and very fast Lister-Jaguar.

Jack Brabham, perhaps reflecting on his win at the previous meeting, said, 'I think Crystal Palace is a very exciting little circuit. I prefer a circuit with many bends and corners as there is not much schooling required for driving down long straights. . .'

Ian Walker, a relative newcomer to racing, said, 'I enjoy driving at the Palace not only because I have had a certain amount of success there (I also had an accident there three years ago) but because the surroundings are so pleasant and the crowd so enthusiastic. The circuit is an interesting one which always provides good close racing. The boys in brown [he was referring to the park keepers who wore smart brown suits and hats] are most helpful and go out of their way to make us welcome. From the spectators' point of view it is most interesting, with a variety of corners and cars lapping at just over a minute. Of all the meetings I go to, Crystal Palace ones are the most pleasant.'

Not all the competitors, it should be said, felt the park keepers were unfailingly welcoming: some found that a minority of them resented 'dirty, noisy racing machines in their nice clean park'. Nonetheless, they welcomed 17,000 spectators into the Palace grounds for that August meeting. It was to be an incident-filled afternoon. With Tommy Bridger (Cooper-Norton) leading the Formula 3 race, it was left to Parker and Cowley to provide a dice for second.

Eventually the two duelling Coopers touched and Cowley's car rolled over twice. When the dust settled the undaunted driver emerged from the wreck, ran back to his road car waiting in the paddock and roared off down the road towards Brands Hatch to drive another racer to third place there! Keith Hall had the most successful afternoon, scoring a hat-trick of wins in his works Lotus.

The Palace was being kept busy in that summer of 1957: on August 10 it hosted an important cycle race and the following week, August 17, 'Bemsee' returned to promote a motorcycle meeting. Despite some big names in the entry list a disappointing crowd of only just over 8,000 turned up. Returning to the scene of his many triumphs was John Surtees, by now reigning 500cc World Champion. He had raced very successfully at Thruxton on the August Bank Holiday Monday and of course he cleaned up at the Palace as well. Three of John's keenest rivals were unable to race, though: Bob McIntyre was still unfit following a recent spill, though present to spectate; Geoff Monty was away on business; and Cecil Sandford, 250cc World Champion, had given up his rapid FB Mondial for the day to marry his fiancee Patricia, daughter of his long-time sponsor Arthur Taylor.

Many machines again had fully enclosing fairings, although the riders agreed there was no real advantage on a twisty circuit like the Palace. Geoff Tanner said his Norton kept the fairing on simply because it now felt strange to race without it. Surtees dominated the 250cc, 350cc and 500cc races and set three new lap records. In the Senior race, three riders were injured in a crash during Heat 2 – Bernard Codd hurt his leg, John Hempleman his collar-bone and Ginger Payne his wrist. Peter Ferbrache won the heat, Surtees having taken Heat 1. In the final, the interest centred on who would finish second. Surtees on his Norton disappeared into the distance, and behind him came Alastair King (Norton), Peter Murphy (Matchless), John Clark (Norton), then the Nortons of Derek Minter and Peter Ferbrache. The latter pair began picking off the riders ahead of them, and on lap 11 Minter took second place from Alastair King at Ramp Bend. Ferbrache tried to follow but was unable to pass King before the chequered flag. In winning, Surtees left the 500cc lap record at 79.43mph. It was a similar story in the 350cc race. Alastair King (Norton) won Heat 1, John Clark (Norton) Heat 2 and Surtees Heat 3. As Surtees led the final away it was left to Peter Murphy to hang on to second place on his AJS, although King put in a spirited chase after a poor start. Clark, Ferbrache, Minter and Tanner all disputed the placings, but Clark lost any chance of success when he caught a footrest on the track at South Tower and was thrown off.

In the 250cc race John Surtees wheeled out a three-year-old NSU Sportmax and lapped the entire field bar Dick Harding's Velocette. Dave Chadwick won the 125cc race on his MV, an excellent result for a man who had never raced at the Palace before, and Fred Launchberry won the 50cc event on an Itom. The most closely fought event turned out to be the sidecar race, won by Pip Harris from the scrapping Norton outfits of Jackie Beeton and Bill Boddice, the latter, troubled with gear-selection difficulties, eventually surrendering third place to Alan Young on another Norton outfit. But there was no doubt that it was the remarkable domination of John Surtees, the two-wheeler king of Crystal Palace, that the racegoers would remember from that sunny August afternoon.

So the 1957 season came to an early close. When it was all totted up, the LCC's total income from the circuit that year had been £19,770, with expenses of £17,408 leaving a profit of £2,362: racing was popular and it made the council money too.

It seemed a long break for the fans till Easter Monday, April 7, 1958, when the circuit came to life again. The ACU South Eastern Centre were in charge, and announced that entry fees would be returned to all starters at this meeting. The previous year they had given part of the fee back and before that they had refunded fees in full to all finishers. It was a warm gesture from the organizers but a cold weekend from the weather gods. Saturday practice was abandoned because snow fell. Fortunately it thawed by Monday but a chill in the air remained, though it did not deter the faithful, just over 16,000 of whom came through the gates to watch. John Surtees was not there, but a new rising star was – Mike Hailwood. Having made his debut the previous year at the age of 17, Mike was embarking on his first full season, with backing from his well-off motorcycle dealer father. Young 'Mike the Bike' was set to cause a sensation during 1958, winning nearly 60 races, setting 38 lap and race records and

taking three out of four ACU Road Racing Stars. Palace racegoers had an early glimpse of his devastating form as he scored an easy win in the 200cc race and set a new record of 68.55mph on his MV Agusta. He was also taken before the Clerk of the Course for a reprimand because he had been caught passing his paddock tickets over the fence for his friends to gain free admission – Dad Hailwood was furious and duly gave the Clerk of the Course a reprimand of his own! Equally dominating in the 250cc final, Mike took the lead on lap 2 and that was the last the opposition saw of his NSU.

In the 350cc event, Derek Minter (Norton) was in control just as convincingly. By lap 4 he was into North Tower Crescent before the second-place man L Flury (AJS) had left South Tower. Flury eventually dropped his bike, letting Brian Setchell take second on his Norton after a dice with Tony Thorp's similar machine and Lurcock's AJS. Minter took the Senior race too, after Peter Ferbrache and Bruce Daniels (all three were on Nortons) had briefly scrapped for the lead. Ferbrache and Daniels tried very hard to stay with Minter and were not far away at the chequered flag, Ferbrache setting fastest lap in the process. Veteran Jackie Beeton won the sidecar race.

If there had been a long gap between the last bike race of 1957 and the 1958 season opener, the car racing fans had

The unlimited-capacity sports cars could be relied upon to provide an impressive display of racing at Crystal Palace during what is generally considered to have been a golden era for these cars. Here an HWM-Jaguar leads a pair of DB3S Aston Martins and three more Jaguar-powered cars through South Tower Corner.

Bruce Halford's HWM-Jaguar taking the lead ahead of two Aston Martin DB3Ss and a Lister-Jaguar at the approach to Ramp Bend.

The registration number always identified the make of this sports-racing car. Originally driven mainly by George Abecassis, John Heath's partner in HW Motors, it was later handled by a variety of drivers, including Les Leston, then earned considerable fame late in its career with Johnny Bekaert at the wheel.

waited even longer. On Whit Monday, May 26, the BARC returned to the Palace. London was in the grip of a bus strike, which may have contributed to keeping attendance low at 13,367. It was a meeting full of incident. Keith Hall crashed his Lotus 11 at Ramp Bend in practice, breaking some ribs and sustaining a spinal injury, and J D Lewis wrote off his Cooper. During racing, Tim Parnell lost control of his Cooper-Climax, cleared a 10-foot earth bank and ended up in the infield, fortunately without injury. Formula 2 cars provided the mainstay of the meeting and heat winners were Ivor Bueb (Lotus-Climax) and Ken Tyrrell, the Formula 1 team owner of later years driving one of Alan Brown's Cooper-Climax cars alongside Carroll Shelby. The final was another thrilling Palace race, led for the first eight laps by Ian Burgess (Cooper-Climax) before George Wicken, also in a Cooper-Climax, took over and Burgess fell back into the clutches of a snarling pack composed of Tommy Bridger and Bruce McLaren in Coopers and Ivor Bueb's Lotus. These four continued to swap places until Bueb slowed with transmission bothers. Up front, Wicken was in trouble with a broken valve spring and on lap 22 he was engulfed by his pursuers. At the line Ian Burgess was first, 0.8sec ahead of Tommy Bridger, with McLaren third just over 2sec behind. Ivor Bueb brought his ailing Lotus in fourth.

Tommy Bridger took some consolation from winning the Formula 3 race, after the lead had changed hands five times, from Don Parker with Ian Raby third. Bridger and Parker had the ubiquitous Cooper-Nortons, Raby a Flash-Special Norton. As in Formula 2 and 3, so in the sports car classes, Cooper and Lotus were the names dominating the entry list, and Alan Stacey's Lotus took a fairly dull final from that of Innes Ireland. Stacey had won the first heat, but the second had provided more excitement and variety as John Brown in the works Elva-Climax led from Randall's Lotus. Chris Summers (Arden-Climax) gave chase and took the lead on lap 7, lost it a lap later and regained it again just before the finish. Only a second covered the first three places.

Formula 2 cars reappeared at the Palace in July for the BRSCC meeting, but the crowd was disappointing – perhaps a lot of people were away on holiday – only 6,500 turning up to see Syd Jensen (Cooper) winning from Ivor Bueb (Cooper) and Jim Russell (Cooper). Though it was still peak holiday time, twice the number of spectators attended the next meeting, motorcycle racing organized by 'Bemsee' on August 4, Bank Holiday Monday, the first time since the war that bikes had occupied this prestigious date. Trying to ensure close racing, the organizers had dispensed with the usual heats and finals, and divided the 350cc,

In pursuit of sidecar race winner Bill Boddice, T Folwell and P M Knocker and their Matchless (6) hold a narrow lead over the Norton of L W Taylor and P Glover (9) as they emerge from Ramp Bend during the May 1957 meeting.

Senior and sidecar classes into races for 'expert' and 'non-expert' graded categories. The 350 experts provided many of the best thrills as Bruce Daniels and Ned Minihan diced on their Nortons to finish one and two. Five more riders were swapping places behind them, Frank Perris and Ernie Washer eventually emerging third and fourth to complete a Norton quartet. Also Norton-mounted was Mike Hailwood who had been badly baulked at the start, lost a lot of ground in consequence and did well to finish sixth with his engine misfiring badly. Bruce Daniels and Frank Perris, both on Nortons, also had a good scrap in the 500cc experts race, Daniels eventually getting away and Ned Minihan, yet another Norton rider, just pipping Perris for second on the line. Mike Hailwood won the 250cc race on an NSU and behind him was another young man beginning to make his mark in motorcycle racing, Phil Read.

A car race meeting originally fixed for August 16 was cancelled, so the season ended on an autumnal note on October 4 with another 'Bemsee' Club Day held in windy conditions with the track dampened liberally by bursts of heavy rain. Neither Alan Trow nor Derek Minter was able to start, so it was left to Mike Hailwood to mop up the spoils, if not the rain-soaked track. Mike the Bike lapped almost the entire field to win the 125cc race on his Ducati,

and he also took wins in the 250cc event (FB Mondial) and the 1,000cc race (Norton). In the 350cc race he was leading when the heavens opened, causing him to ease his pace. Ginger Payne saw the opportunity and took the lead on his Norton, pulling out a gap of 100 yards. But he tried a little too hard and with half a lap left he lost it on the slippery track, dropped his bike and handed victory back to Hailwood. To add variety and interest, a vintage race was included in the programme, evoking memories of earlier days at the Palace. Howard German rode his 1929 Velocette 250 to a win – remarkably, his lap speed was only about 5mph down on Hailwood's time on the 250cc FB Mondial, the latest in racing machinery in 1958.

If the season closed on a somewhat wet and dreary note, the 1959 season was to get off to a tragic start with the usual Easter Monday opening meeting on March 30, this time run by the ACU South Eastern Centre. The day dawned bright and fresh and the first few races passed without incident. Dave Chadwick won the 200cc race, breaking the race record and bettering Hailwood's lap record by almost 2mph in spite of losing 12 seconds at the start and leaving the grid in last place. Chadwick also won his 250cc heat on his MV, while Ned Minihan's Velocette took the other. In the final Chadwick was unable to get his MV to fire at the first attempt and was again left badly, but his riding ability enabled him to catch and pass Minihan to take the lead on the sixth lap, with a best lap time only 0.2sec short of John Surtees' record. But luck was against him as his gearbox seized, leaving the victory to Minihan. The 350cc heats went to Minihan (on a Norton this time) and Bruce Daniels, but Peter Ferbrache (AJS) emerged victorious in the final.

Tragedy struck in the first heat of the 1,000cc race. On lap 3, after a clean start, the riders were approaching Ramp Bend when Edward Boarer (Norton) hit the sleeper barrier and was pitched from his machine which landed on top of him, causing fatal injuries. Those closely following were unable to miss the stricken bike. Peter Luscombe was thrown into the air when his Triumph hit the wreckage, the impact dislodged his crash helmet and he too was fatally injured. The BSA of G J Griffen was another machine involved, both bike and rider somersaulting and landing on the track. J C Fagence (Velocette) received concussion and J Wheeler (Velocette) broke his collar-bone. The race was quickly stopped, and marshals, doctors and first-aid men rushed to the scene of the crash. When the carnage had been cleared the meeting resumed, but the accident cast a terrible shadow over the rest of the afternoon. Joe Dunphy won the re-run of the ill-fated first heat on his 650 Norton-Triumph, while the other heats went to Ned Minihan and Peter Ferbrache, both on G50 Matchless machines.

Ferbrache also took the final, but to add yet more gloom to the proceedings Minihan fell at Ramp, fortunately without injury, and further down the field K Purchase (Norton-Triumph) broke his collar-bone and M J G Brown (Triumph) broke his leg. Events had conspired to make both racing and spectating a dismal affair, and no-one was sorry when the last race had been run and it was time to depart for home.

As is usual when a fatality occurs in motor sport, the popular press devoted a lot of space to the incident. The front page of the next day's *Daily Mirror* showed a picture of the unfortunate Griffen and his BSA cartwheeling through the air, with the headline 'He Lived', and the centre spread depicted the whole grisly scene in detail, captioned 'Bank Holiday Horror', with riders and machines identified with arrows and a graphic description of the terrible events of that day.

On Whit Monday, May 18, 1959, the BRSCC were promoting the meeting, the main race of which was the London Trophy for Formula 2 cars. For that event almost the entire entry was either Cooper or Lotus and all were powered by the Coventry Climax engine with the exception of two Borgward-engined Coopers entered by the British Racing Partnership for George Wicken and Ivor Bueb. And

Scene for the last time. The August 1960 motorcycle meeting marked the final occasion when races at Crystal Palace were started from the straight connecting the New Link with Ramp Bend. Immediately afterwards the track was closed to racing for several months while major construction work began on the new National Sports Centre.

View from the bridge over Ramp Bend as a field of (mainly Lotus) sports-racing cars streams uphill through Maxim Rise towards South Tower Corner.

A famous name in a less familiar guise in 1958. Ken Tyrrell drove a Formula 2 Cooper to considerable effect before he decided that he was unlikely to become World Champion unless he concentrated on team management and, eventually, Formula 1 car construction. With Jackie Stewart's help, Tyrrell duly won the Constructor's Championship for the first time in 1971.

Ronnie Moore working hard in the roomy cockpit of his Formula 2 Cooper during a race in May 1958. In those days, before a wave of safety-consciousness enveloped motor racing, bare arms were the norm, and there was little protection, either, for marshals or photographers at the trackside.

it was Coopers that took the honours, Roy Salvadori in a Climax-powered car winning from Bueb, with another Cooper-Climax, that of Chris Bristow, in third place. Salvadori also took a win in the Norbury Trophy race for sports cars, driving a 2.5-litre Cooper-Maserati entered by John Coombs. A works Lotus-Climax was second in the hands of an up-and-coming British driver being rewarded for his hard work as a mechanic for Colin Chapman's fledgling Team Lotus. His name was Graham Hill.

Hill also appeared in the Touring Car race at the same meeting. It was the first time the Crystal Palace spectators had seen the sort of cars many of them drove every day being used in competition. Graham Hill had formed Speedwell Conversions with Len Adams, John Sprinzel and George Hulbert in 1957, each man contributing £25. With its £100 working capital, the small tuning firm set about converting ordinary Morris Minors and Austin A35s into surprisingly quick and nimble cars. To prove their workmanship they raced their own A35s and two were entered at Crystal Palace, one for Hill and one for Adams.

The cars were quite amazing. Capable of nearly 100mph on the straight, they were able to corner with unexpected rapidity too, the drivers throwing them sideways into the bends and scrubbing off excess speed in a haze of burning rubber. Typical grids in the early days of saloon car racing would include Les Leston in a Riley 1.5, Bill Blydenstein in a Borgward Isabella, Bob Jennings in a Renault Dauphine, plus a collection of Morris Minors, Ford Prefects, Wolseley 1500s and the recently introduced Austin A40s. The bigger capacity class would comprise Jaguars, Ford Zephyrs, MG Magnettes and the like. Saloon car racing proved very popular with racegoers able to relate their own cars to those performing on the track, and it would grow throughout the 1960s and 70s to become the sophisticated, large-budget formula it is today. At Crystal Palace it rarely failed to produce close and spectacular racing and there were some memorable tussles in the ensuing years.

The motorcycle racing fraternity returned to the Palace on August 3, 1959, no doubt with some anxiety following the Easter disaster. 'Bemsee' laid on a 12-race meeting for

Saloon car racing, 1958-style. Here a Mark 2 Ford Zephyr leads an Austin A35, an MG Magnette, another A35, a Fiat and a Borgward through South Tower Corner.

In those days, production car racing really did mean racing cars in (more or less) road trim. No doubt this Hillman Minx and Ford Anglia were driven to the circuit, and then driven home again.

the benefit of 17,000 spectators. The programme described the entry list as 'just the right ingredients' and the Crystal Palace circuit as 'just the right mixing bowl', picking out some of the competitors as a 'sample of the menu'! Fortunately, culinary metaphors notwithstanding, nobody made a hash of it and the meeting passed without serious incident. Phil Read added to his fast growing reputation with a win on his Norton in the 350cc race.

There was just one more car race meeting planned for 1959, and the BARC took charge on August 22. Practice was marked by a spate of wheel-shedding which saw several competitors coming to grief but without serious injury. The main event was the August Trophy race for sports cars, to be run in two heats and a final. Eric Broadley's amazing 1,100cc Lola was the car to beat, two works examples being entered for Peter Gammon and Peter Ashdown. Main opposition would come from the works Lotus 17s of Alan Stacey and Michael Taylor, but there were also the works Elvas and several private Lotus entries to consider, as well as a Kieft, a Tojeiro and others. Lola was a comparative newcomer on the scene but so successful had the cars proved that Eric Broadley had recently given up his job as a building-site manager to concentrate on making racing cars instead. Today, of course, the marque is one of the most respected names in racing car construction, having enjoyed huge success in sports car racing as well as single-seaters from Formula Ford to Grand Prix and Indianapolis cars. On this occasion it was a Lola that took the first heat, Gammon leading Arundell's Lotus across the line. Colin Chapman's team took Heat 2, Stacey beating Ashdown's Lola into second place. But the works Lola cars were first and second in the final, with Peter Gammon winning from Peter Ashdown. Alan Stacey upheld Lotus honour with third place and Peter Arundell came home fourth in his privately entered Lotus. Amongst the supporting events was a scratch race for prewar racing cars and once again the Palace reverberated to the sound of supercharged Maseratis, ERAs and the like, the winner being an ERA driven by D Hull.

The next motor sport event at the Palace was not until Saturday, November 21, a late date and something rather different for the London racegoers as the circuit was to host the final stage of the RAC Rally. Eleven scratch races were to be held, and a wide variety of near-standard family saloons and a few sports cars, a typical rallying entry of the 1950s, arrived in the chill autumn air. There were Austin A35s, Sprites, Riley 1.5s, Sunbeam Rapiers and Volvos – and a Wolseley 1500 which caused a few scares among the officials with its spectacular progress, its driver apparently trying to live up to his name, C Bent-Marshall!

As the last few months of the decade passed, news of coming alterations at Crystal Palace began to appear in the motoring press. Sir Isaac Howard, leader of the London County Council, had announced that the summer of 1960 could see the start of construction of the National Youth and Sports Centre within the Crystal Palace park. Administration of the scheme was entrusted to the Central Council for Physical Recreation, and in *The Motor Cycle* 'Nitor' wrote of his anxiety that this body might not look on motor sport in a favourable light. 'The area is big enough for both a race and athletics crowd,' he wrote, 'but conflicts could arise.' Urging the ACU and RAC to press the claims of the Palace as a motor sporting venue, he warned, 'a road racing circuit in the heart of London is an asset we certainly cannot afford to lose.'

The history of Crystal Palace race circuit is not entirely about racing. On this occasion the inside of South Tower Corner was used for a static display of immaculately presented vehicles at a Vintage and Veteran Car Rally.

CHAPTER 6

Crystal Palace in racing's golden era

Stars shine on two, three and four wheels, 1960 to 1969

As the new decade opened, Britain moved forward into the 1960s full of hope for a bright future. With the days of postwar austerity behind him, the average man in the street now had more time and money than ever before to spend on leisure and recreation, and that included sport, both as spectator and participant. Almost ten years earlier, the idea of developing Crystal Palace into more than a motor racing track had first been mooted, and Sir Gerald Barry, who had been director-general of the Festival of Britain in 1951, which itself was in part a celebration of the centenary of the Great Exhibition in Hyde Park, was invited to submit a scheme for the redevelopment of the site. He envisaged the construction of a National Sports and Leisure Centre, plans were drawn up and much discussion ensued. The go-ahead was eventually given and in June 1960 work began on the complex, which was designed, in the words of the slogan the London County Council would use in their promotion of the new-look Crystal Palace, to offer 'Sport for All'.

Some £2,750,000 was spent on the centre by the time it was officially opened by HRH Prince Philip, Duke of Edinburgh, in 1964. Since then, progressive improvements have continued to add more facilities for spectators and competitors alike and today it is probably the best known athletics stadium in Britain. The project utilized much of the infield area of the motor racing circuit, the athletics track and seating for 17,000 occupying the old speedway area and being equipped in 1968 with the first 'Tartan' synthetic surface in Europe, something which was of great benefit for the British team training for the Mexico Olympics of that year. Other outdoor facilities included practice areas for track and field events, a floodlit arena for soccer, rugby and American football, grass and synthetic pitches for hockey, football and five-a-side soccer, six tennis courts and an artificial ski-slope. Indoors was provision for netball, basketball, volleyball, squash, badminton, cricket practice, judo, karate and a variety of other activities. Swimming and diving pools with underwater observation windows as well as training halls and superbly equipped gymnasiums were part of the comprehensive specification. Included too were a residential tower block, facilities to entertain guests at sponsored events, halls which could be hired for exhibitions and conferences, licensed bars, restaurants and cafeterias.

It was a very impressive development, an important new resource for the capital city, and did much to live up to its claim to provide sport for all – although ultimately at the expense of motor sport, for, as 'Nitor' had sensed, there was a clash of style and aspirations if not an actual conflict over accommodation between the two kinds of sport, and the opening of the new centre can perhaps be seen as the beginning of the end for the motor racing circuit. Certainly the grounds of the Palace were transformed during the construction, and many famous landmarks disappeared as the contractors' equipment moved in.

But motor sport still had a long way to go, and the new season began in the traditional way with the ACU meeting on Easter Monday, April 18, 1960. In the programme introduction, Bob Holliday, editor of *Motor Cycling*, wrote of the 'friendly, matey reputation' which Crystal Palace had become known for, and evidently the crowds agreed, for some 27,000 paying spectators arrived. They were rewarded with some good, close racing, although there were few big names on the entry list. Mick O'Rourke was riding Hermann Meier's Ariel Arrow and took a heat win, but could only manage third in the final behind Hardy's NSU and Rowe's Norton. Bob Rowe took 350cc honours from Brian Setchell (both on Nortons), but the real entertainment came from the similar machine of Ned Minihan who scythed through the field to take third and set fastest lap after a bad start. Minihan and Rowe enjoyed another close dice throughout the 500cc race, the former finally getting a win and another fastest lap into the bargain. Ted Young and J McAuliffe won the sidecar race on their ETY Vincent.

The year's first car races were at the customary Whit Monday meeting, which fell on June 6, 1960. The morning was sunny and warm and nearly 30,000 spectators turned up. No doubt many were hoping to see the new young Scottish star Jim Clark, entered by Team Lotus in both the main Formula 2 event and the Formula Junior race. Unfortunately he was unable to race and so Trevor Taylor deputized for him; for Taylor it was a lucky break as he had a most successful meeting. He took the Lotus to a Formula Junior heat win despite the challenge of Henry Taylor who was driving Ken Tyrrell's Cooper-Austin. In Heat 2, Keith Ballisat, driving a second, similar Tyrrell entry, had a spirited tussle with Colin Andrews (Lotus) until he spun leaving Ramp Bend. Andrews was unable to avoid the Cooper and received nasty facial cuts which needed hospital treatment. R N Prior (Lola) inherited the win from the two sidelined cars. Trevor Taylor proved unbeatable in the final.

The sunny morning had turned into a rainy afternoon and the 36-lap Crystal Palace Trophy race for Formula 2 cars was run on a wet track. Trevor Taylor had been fastest in practice but George Wicken's bright red Cooper-Climax made a storming start from the second row to grab an early lead. Taylor squeezed past on lap 2 and stayed in front to the end. Wicken tried to hold on but had an alarming spin and retired soon after.

An entertaining saloon car race had been led by Les Leston in his Volvo 122S until he was black-flagged for a loose exhaust pipe, leaving Alan Hutchinson (Riley 1.5) to take the honours. Team Speedwell's entry for Les Adams in this race was not the usual A35 but a new car just beginning to show its huge potential in competition, as well as its universal appeal to the public, an 848cc Austin Mini Se7en. The other supporting race, delayed by a downpour just before the start, once again showed how good the Lola-Climax sports car was, Peter Ashdown's works entry leading from start to finish.

July 2 saw Crystal Palace stage the Guinness Trophy Meeting, organized by 'Bemsee'. It was a good day for Ned Minihan who won both 350cc and 1,000cc finals on his Nortons, not without a struggle in the smaller capacity event. He made a very poor start allowing Tom Thorp and the ex-scrambler Ron Langston, both on AJS bikes, to gain a big lead. Minihan had to fight his way through the field in company with Mick O'Rourke (Norton), and this pair were in fifth and sixth place by the third lap, with Langston and Thorp still neck and neck up at the front. That dice ended on lap 6 when Langston tried just a bit too hard and crashed spectacularly, fortunately without injury. Two laps later, Minihan took the lead from Thorp with some masterly riding, whilst third place was being disputed by O'Rourke,

A close battle between Ken Whorlow (MV Agusta) and Mick O'Rourke (Ariel Arrow) enlivened the crowd at the Bank Holiday Monday motorcycle race meeting in 1961. Above, W J Hicks gets hard on the brakes of his BSA on the approach to North Tower Crescent at the same meeting.

Getting down to it. Ivor Webb tries to minimize the wind resistance aboard his Itom during the first race for 50cc machines at Crystal Palace.

Setchell (Norton) and Young (AJS). Thorp had not given up and on lap 11, braking hard and late, he was alongside Minihan at Ramp Bend. But Minihan used all the Norton's power to out-accelerate him up Maxim Rise, held the lead for the remaining four laps and eventually beat Thorp by 40 yards. Tom had the consolation of beating John Surtees' three-year-old lap record with a speed of 76.98mph, and Mick O'Rourke took the third place from Setchell and Lewis. Minihan repeated his win in the senior race, though he did not have to work quite so hard, leading from flag to flag despite some pressure from Ron Langston who was never more than a few seconds behind. Mike Hailwood's lap record was equalled in an impressive performance by Ken Whorlow (MV) in the 125cc event, and Fred Hardy (NSU) took the 250cc race when the expected challenge from O'Rourke's Ariel Arrow failed to materialize. Ted Young trounced the sidecar opposition, and the crowd were also entertained by something a little different in the form of a six-lap race for production motor-scooters won by J B Gamble on a Maico. A Heinkel ridden by Don Noys into second place was the same machine ridden by Peter Humber to win the scooter class in the Welsh Two-Day Trial.

Construction work on the Sports Centre meant an early finish to racing for the 1960 season, so Bank Holiday Monday, August 1, saw the final meeting of the year, and was also the last time the circuit would be used with the start-finish line on the bottom straight. It was a showery day which made the track slippery. The programme began with a win for Howard German on his Sheene Special in the 50cc race; further down the field, finishing ninth, was a young Bill Ivy on a Chisholm-Itom. Phil Read, aged just 21, showed superb form by winning the 350cc race on his Norton despite being last away from the start. He also looked unbeatable on his 500cc Norton, but the riders contesting second place, George Young (Norton) and Chris Williams (Norton-powered Matchless G50), collided at Ramp Bend, and the red flag was shown to allow an ambulance onto the track for them, though neither was badly hurt. In the re-run, shortened to eight laps, Read once again took the lead, but before the first lap was completed Ned Minihan tried to pass him at Park Curve, failed and had to step off his machine. Six riders behind him came to grief as they took evasive action, and the ambulance was on the track again to collect the only casualty, Joe Dunphy, who was concussed. As it was getting late the meeting had to end on this rather abrupt note, and as the spectators left the circuit they no doubt felt that Phil Read was the moral victor.

Now that the contractors could occupy the whole park and really get on with the new sports complex, the racing circuit started to be altered as part of the redevelopment. The athletics arena began to take shape on the site of the old paddock and the bridge at Ramp Bend was demolished. So too was the famous bridge over the Terrace Straight, and the track there was widened by 5 feet, to 35 feet, to accommodate the new starting grid. North Tower Crescent was resurfaced, the camber on the outside being raised several inches. The spectator banking along the Terrace Straight was improved by the addition of open seating, those familiar grey-painted wooden chairs being laid out in their hundreds. New pits were constructed on the inside of Terrace Straight and behind them a spacious five-acre paddock, which would become the envy of many other circuits, was laid out, a new brick toilet block making facilities for the competitor among the best in the country. A new footbridge led people over the circuit at Maxim Rise from the Low Level Station to the infield and also to the emerging Sports Centre. But vehicles going into the paddock now had to cross the circuit through gates from Ledrington Road, just before South Tower Corner. This meant delays when racing or practice were in progress, but a new bridge would have been both impractical and expensive. Bad weather put the work behind schedule but the season opened as planned on Easter Monday, April 3, 1961, with the ACU National Meeting.

'A new look for the Crystal Palace circuit – starting today!' So the programme for the meeting introduced spectators to the alterations made during the winter. The new look was well accepted, too, and many who had felt that the track was threatened by the Sports Centre were pleased to see all the new facilities the LCC had provided for the motor racing fraternity. Perhaps things weren't so gloomy for the future of the circuit – even though the weather was. It was more than April showers, the rain fell all day, leaving the track surface glistening and very treacherous. Fortunately there were few mishaps, though many riders retired with waterlogged ignition systems, including Palace expert and 350cc favourite Ned Minihan. It was an unknown rider who was the star of the show, Ted Wooder winning his 350cc heat on an AJS and only narrowly being beaten into second place in the final by the similar machine of Robin Dawson. Wooder swapped to a Matchless to win his 500cc heat and was leading the final until lap 6 when the far more experienced Joe Dunphy (Norton) passed him, and he then managed to hang on to second despite fierce pressure from Dawson. Another to triumph over the difficult conditions was Fred Hardy: with his steamed-up goggles pushed down to his chin he won the 125cc and 250cc races, both times on an MV.

On Whit Monday, May 22, it was the turn of the car drivers to try the new-look Palace. The BRSCC had laid on an excellent programme with a fine entry, the main race being the 37-lap London Trophy for Formula 1 cars. It was no surprise that Roy Salvadori should win this, starting from pole position in his Yeoman Credit Racing Cooper-Climax, the team being managed by Reg Parnell, now retired from driving but remembered with great affection by the Palace fans. Henry Taylor brought his UDT-Laystall Lotus-Climax home second. Many people had come to see the debut of the sensational new Jaguar E-Type, two having been entered in the Norbury Trophy race, one by Equipe Endeavour for Jack Sears (that team also had a Ferrari Berlinetta for Mike Parkes) and one by John Coombs for Roy Salvadori. They proved unbeatable, finishing one and two and giving Salvadori another win. He also won *The Green Helmet* Trophy race, named after a forthcoming MGM film with a motor racing theme, in a Yeoman Credit Cooper-Climax sports car, as well as the saloon car race in John Coombs' Jaguar 3.8, and so at the end of the day had won every race he started. The only other winner was Alan Rees (Lotus-Ford) in the Formula Junior race, with Mike Parkes second in the Chequered Flag Gemini-Ford. The entry included Bernie Ecclestone (Elva), Denny Hulme (Cooper), Mike Spence (Emeryson) and Frank Gardner

Mike Spence, driving for Ian Walker Racing, leads Team Lotus works driver Alan Rees into the shadows at North Tower Crescent in their Lotus-Ford 20s during the London Trophy race for Formula Junior cars in September 1962.

A crowded grid and crowded terraces. Riders and machines lined up on the Terrace Straight starting grid for the 1963 August Bank Holiday meeting, which was dominated by Joe Dunphy, who completed a clean sweep by winning the 250cc, 350cc and 500cc races.

Following a severe winter, there were few leaves on the trees when the season started with a motorcycle meeting in April. The sloping ground on the outside of North Tower Crescent provides a natural vantage point for spectators watching the first lap of one of the solo races.

A busy paddock scene for the June 1963 meeting with four Minis already in the marshalling area for their saloon race while Formula Junior cars are being worked on in the background in preparation for their Anerley Trophy race.

(Lotus), all men on the way to make a name for themselves in motor racing.

A family name well known to Palace motorcycle fans was on the entry list for the 'Bemsee' Bank Holiday meeting on August 7, 1961, when Norman Surtees, enjoying his first full racing season, arrived to carry on the tradition of his father Jack and brother John. Many of the stars had been attracted away to rival meetings at Thruxton and Oulton Park, but with glorious summer weather it was a day for the clubmen and the London racegoers to savour. No less than five lap records were broken by, amongst others, Roy Nicholson on his DRC-Itom in the 50cc race and Chris Williams who shattered the vintage record on his Scott. As a foretaste of the Japanese invasion later in the 1960s, Bob Rowe rode a race-modified Honda-Benley 125cc to take the lap record on his way to second place just a fifth of a second behind Fred Hardy's MV. Unfortunately, Rowe's day was soured when he dropped his 250cc Velocette at North Tower and was taken to hospital with a broken ankle. Ned Minihan had his usual successful Palace outing, winning both the 350cc race on his AJS and the last race, the 500cc event, by only a few yards on his Norton after a furious dice with Robin Dawson and Ernie Wooder, both on Matchless machines. Brian Osbourne also had a good day with two

wins, in the second 350cc race on his AJS and in the 250cc race. The Ariel Arrow of Mick O'Rourke had looked favourite for that event when the pursuing MV Agusta of Ken Whorlow retired with a broken piston, but Osbourne rode his NSU Sportmax with such flair that even the experienced O'Rourke could not hold him.

The final meeting of 1961 came a month later with the BARC in charge on September 2. Good weather but a very small crowd of just 6,011 greeted the competitors. The main event was the September Trophy for Formula Junior cars. Heat 1 went to Dennis Taylor in his privately entered Lola-Ford and namesake Trevor Taylor won the second heat in the works Lotus-Ford. The 25-lap final saw the two Taylors dicing for the lead, the Lola leading for eight laps before the Lotus took over and went on to win by some 3½ seconds. Sports car races were among the supporting events, but perhaps the most entertainment was derived from an invitation scratch race for prewar cars, reminding older spectators of the Palace in earlier years. H S Clifford stalled his supercharged Alta and received a helpful push start from the Scuderia Rossa Invicta driven by Morin Scott! Dudley Gahagan's ERA took the lead but slowed with trouble on the penultimate lap, allowing the similar car of Alan Cottam to pass and win. As Gahagan crossed the line to claim second place the ERA caught fire but fortunately the flames were extinguished quickly without too much damage. Though now painted red and fitted with a 2-litre engine, Gahagan's car was the machine that Arthur Dobson had driven in prewar days, when it had been white and in 1½-litre form, in those memorable races with Bira at the Palace.

As each winter passed, more work was completed on the National Sports Centre, and as the enthusiasts gathered on the terraces on April 23, 1962, for the Easter Monday meeting they were able to see just how impressive the new construction would be. The race programme promised 'never a dull moment at a Crystal Palace meeting' but the weather was dull, with intermittent drizzle most of the day. It did not stop Joe Dunphy, however, the Norton rider taking both the 500cc final and the 350cc race, despite a valiant effort by Palace expert and 1961 Senior Manx Grand Prix winner Ned Minihan (Norton) who equalled the lap record at 76.98mph. Dunphy then equalled the five-year-old 500cc record of John Surtees at 79.43mph. The Surtees name stayed in the record book as Norman took both a win and a lap record in the 125cc race on his Bultaco. Fred Hardy, too, was a winner on the 250cc REG twin built locally by Bob Geeson.

The late Easter date meant that June 11 was the next Bank Holiday for the BARC to promote a national meeting,

with Formula 1 cars topping the bill. BRM and Coventry Climax had both developed new V8 engines for the 1½-litre Grand Prix formula which had come into effect in 1961 and many London racegoers were anxious to see and hear these new machines. Roy Salvadori was favourite to win in his Bowmaker Racing Lola-Climax V8, but despite starting from pole position he was unable to compete with a brilliant Innes Ireland who came from the back of the grid in his UDT-Laystall Lotus-BRM V8 and chopped nearly 2½ seconds off the lap record of Salvadori and Henry Taylor to leave it at 57.2 seconds, 87.46mph. Salvadori had to settle for second place whilst Bruce McLaren brought the works Cooper-Climax home third ahead of the Emeryson of Tony Settember and the Lotus-Fords of Brian Hart and David Piper. Salvadori did get his customary Palace win, in a 3.8 Jaguar in the saloon car race, and Australian Paul Hawkins took sports car honours at the wheel of Ian Walker's Lotus 23.

The Anerley Trophy for Formula Junior was decided over two heats and a final, and John Love won the first heat in Ken Tyrrell's Cooper-Austin from the Lotus-Fords of Mike Spence and Alan Rees. Chris Ashmore in the Lawrencetune Elva-Ford took Heat 2 from McKinney (Cooper) and Pike (Ausper). The final saw the works Lotus of Alan Rees win from the Ian Walker car of Mike Spence.

Muscle power before horsepower. The crews of the nine combinations starting the eight-lap sidecar race at the opening 1964 meeting get up speed before letting in their clutches. A bit of a traffic jam seems to be developing!

Equipe Elva driver Steve Minoprio escaped unharmed after his 1,100cc sports car slid off the track during the Anerley Trophy race in September 1963 and came to rest narrowly missing a tree. Here the driver seems to be counting the cost of the torn bodywork.

Right, the Norbury Trophy race for GT cars at the same meeting with Brian Hetreed's Aston Martin DB4GT Zagato narrowly leading Dick Protheroe's Jaguar E-Type and John Miles' Turner.

John Love was third, and in fourth place was a marque new to motor racing that year, the Repco-Brabham driven by a young New Zealand driver, Denny Hulme, who had been sponsored as a 'Driver to Europe' by his compatriots. Five years later, in 1967, the combination would reach the very top, Hulme becoming World Champion in a Repco-Brabham Grand Prix car.

On August 6 'Bemsee' was back in charge, and rain falling on the South London area ensured low speeds and a quiet day's racing. Robin Dawson fought hard to bring his AJS home first in the 350cc race from Chris Williams who almost lost his mount on several occasions, and Joe Dunphy was badly delayed when Ernie Wooder dropped his AJS in front of the Norton rider. But Dunphy scored a runaway win in the 500cc race, setting fastest lap as the track dried, though still some 7mph off the record. Alan Thurgood had the most successful meeting with two wins on his Matchless outfit.

Whilst the Sports Centre was being built, only four meetings a year were organized, two for cars and two for motorcycles, so September 1, 1962, saw an abbreviated season brought to a close with a BRSCC meeting. The 25-lap London Trophy race for Formula Junior was the principal event, once again fought out by two young Lotus drivers, with Alan Rees winning in the works car, adding to

his growing reputation at the Palace, and Mike Spence second in the Ian Walker Racing entry. Peter Ashdown was third in his Superspeed Lola and American driver Roy Pike fourth in the Ausper. A varied programme also offered sports cars and saloons, the protagonists ranging from a 5½-litre Chevrolet to 850cc Minis. The historic race which ended the meeting included a car driven by Hon Patrick Lindsay which had been familiar at Crystal Palace in the late 1930s in the hands of Tony Rolt, ERA R5B, originally supplied to Ecurie White Mouse as a companion to Bira's Romulus and hence christened Remus.

The winter of 1962–63 was long and harsh, and like the rest of the country Crystal Palace lay under a blanket of snow for several weeks. Spring came late and Easter Monday, April 15, brought the welcome return of racing with the ACU in charge, celebrating 10 years of the postwar Palace. The race programme contained the first of what would become a popular series of 'Palace Portraits' each describing a competitor successful at the circuit, Joe Dunphy being chosen for the honour first. The 25-year-old lived nearby and had been born of Anglo-Irish parents in Paddington so he was very much a local hero. On this occasion he demonstrated his prowess by winning the 350cc race on a Norton, beating Griff Jenkins (AJS), and the 250cc race on a

Villiers-powered Greeves Silverstone, prepared as usual by Francis Beart. He very nearly won the 500cc race but was beaten by two-tenths of a second by Griff Jenkins, but he did raise the lap record to 76.68mph. Another new lap record went to George Murphy at 72.31mph on a 125cc Bultaco.

Also celebrating the reborn Palace's tenth birthday were the BARC on June 3 with a 50-mile sports car race for the Crystal Palace Trophy. The Cooper Monaco of Roy Salvadori was a predictable leader for the first 25 laps before transmission trouble intervened, leaving the blue-and-white Normand Lotus-Fords of Jim Clark and Mike Beckwith to finish first and second. Trevor Taylor's similar car was heading for third place until he hit the wall at Park Curve. In an entertaining saloon car race, the mighty Ford Galaxie entered by John Willment and driven by Jack Sears vanquished the tyre-smoking 3.8 Jaguars of Roy Salvadori and current World Champion Graham Hill. The Anerley Trophy was again contested by Formula Juniors, and the first heat was led by Frank Gardner's Brabham before the works car of Denny Hulme took over. Richard Attwood's Lola very nearly snatched second and Mike Spence was eliminated after tangling with a young Chris Amon at North Tower Crescent. The silver Roy Winkelmann Racing Lola-Ford driven by Alan Rees dominated the second heat, but he could only manage third in the final as the two Brabhams of Hulme and Gardner diced for the lead, the works car getting the win. David Hobbs was fourth in the Midland Racing Partnership Lola.

The next bank holiday, August 5, again saw Joe Dunphy in unbeatable form, with three wins in as many races. He had to work hardest in the 500cc event, scrapping furiously with Griff Jenkins (Norton) and Roger Hunter (Matchless). On the way he created another Palace first by lapping at over 80mph on his Norton, leaving the lap record at 80.19mph, a speed which would remain unbeaten for seven years. He took a win and a lap record in the 250cc race and the third win after a poor start in the 350cc event.

The fourth and final meeting of 1963 was held by the BRSCC on September 7. Alan Rees, winner of three of the last five Formula Junior races at the Palace, was expected to win, especially after describing the circuit as his favourite, but it was the Gemini-Ford of Roy Pike which led across the line followed by a Lotus driven by Brian Hart, later well known as a tuner and builder of successful competition engines. Rees did get a win in the Anerley Trophy sports car race with the Winkelmann Lotus 23B. Surprise victor in the saloon car race was Mick Cave whose Austin A40 defeated the nimbler Mini-Coopers and the Ford Anglias.

By 1964 the National Sports Centre was open and conflicts between two different types of sport sharing the same venue began to look inevitable. At first the long established motor sports could claim precedence over athletics but far-sighted people began to doubt if this would always be so: there were only a few bank holidays in the year

Crystal Palace stalwart Joe Dunphy and his crew hard at work in the paddock during the August 1964 meeting. He had an outstanding record of victories on the London circuit, but this was not to be one of his most successful outings and he ended the day having failed to win any of his three races.

and the dates for major events would be bound to clash, so would it be possible for the status quo to last? Time would tell, but for now it was business as usual for the ACU on Easter Monday, March 30, the first of five meetings to be held in 1964. While Dave Simmonds broke the two-year-old 125cc lap record of Norman Surtees and won the race on his Tohatsu, it was his namesake John Simmonds on an AJS who took a brilliant first win in the 350cc race beating the two acknowledged Palace masters Joe Dunphy and Griff Jenkins into the bargain. He also took fourth in the 500cc race which fell almost inevitably to Dunphy. A welcome return to the Palace was made by Mick O'Rourke who took third place in the 125cc race on his Honda.

As well as the opening of the Sports Centre, 1964 saw the arrival at the Palace of a young man, virtually unknown in Britain, to race in Formula 2 and start a meteoric climb to the heights in motor racing. Jochen Rindt was an Austrian, born in 1942 of wealthy parents who owned a spice mill. Orphaned at 15 months by a bombing raid on Hamburg, he

had grown up living with his grandparents. The passion for motor racing began early and amongst his friends was Helmut Marko who was also destined to become a racing driver. A wild youth had been spent competing in various unofficial motor sporting contests until the group of friends began to attend organized races. This led to Rindt competing in touring car races with a Simca in the early 1960s, followed by single-seater racing in a Formula Junior Cooper. When he came of age and inherited money from the family business he was able to take his career a stage further: he visited the 1964 Racing Car Show in London and placed an order for a Formula 2 Brabham. The car was ready for Jochen to race over the Whitsun weekend and on the Sunday he took it to Mallory Park for his first ever race in England. He asked Denny Hulme if he could follow him round the Leicestershire circuit to learn it, and having done so, set fastest time in practice. He made a poor start and was then delayed by an incident, but he still finished third behind two established stars, World Champion Jim Clark

This is the sort of scene which brought so many Crystal Palace race spectators back to the circuit time and time again. Closely bunched competitors fighting it out on a picturesque tree-lined track which allowed the most highly skilled to demonstrate their talent to maximum advantage.

and his experienced team-mate Peter Arundell.

The Formula 2 circus then moved south to compete in the London Trophy at Crystal Palace on Whit Monday. The BARC had split the entry into two heats. The first of these was for the drivers presumed to be the fastest and it was Jim Clark who got the initial lead, but by the end of the first lap Graham Hill in the John Coombs Cooper had taken over to stay in front for the whole 20 laps. Behind Clark came Denny Hulme to finish third. Heat 2 was for the 'novices' but included Peter Arundell whose car had expired on the warm-up lap of the first heat. Palace 'King' Alan Rees had the Roy Winkelmann Brabham on pole but next to him was Jochen Rindt in his Brabham, number 21. David Hobbs got the drop from the other front-row position and his Merlyn led for three-quarters of the first lap before Rindt came past. Alan Rees followed the Austrian through into second place and the two cars lapped nose-to-tail, with Rees fully intending to pass Rindt but finding it impossible as the newcomer opposite-locked his dark blue car around the

Palace track. Rindt won but Rees made fastest lap in the chase. The crowd eagerly awaited the final, for the young pretender from Austria was shaking up the establishment and showing that he was no wealthy playboy but a truly talented and brave driver. Graham Hill took pole position on the grid with Rindt and Rees completing the front row, Clark and Hulme behind them.

The flag fell and Rees, with his Palace reputation at stake, shot into the lead. Though this was Hill's first Formula 2 race, he was of course a former World Champion and widely experienced, and he managed to squeeze by the Winkelmann Brabham on lap 2. He seemed set for victory as he began to pull away, but Rindt took Rees on lap 4 and began to reduce the deficit. The leader was by now having some problems because a bracket holding the rear anti-roll bar had broken and the car was understeering badly. Rindt seized his chance to take the lead. Rees closed up on Hill but the ill-handling Cooper was using so much of the road in the corners that, try as he might, he could not find a way past. At the front Rindt made no mistakes and the crowd were treated to a fine display by a driver obviously going places. He set fastest lap and won the race by a second and a half from Hill and a frustrated Rees. Rindt's hand was blistered from changing gear and the soles of his feet were sore from the pedals, but he had won and clearly made his mark. The press gave him a lot of publicity (although one paper next day carried the headline 'Unknown Australian beats Hill at Crystal Palace'). Just a year later, Jochen Rindt shared the winning Ferrari at Le Mans and signed a Formula 1 contract with Cooper. That Palace win also assured him of a warm welcome from London racegoers on his subsequent returns to the circuit where it first became clear he was in the front rank of racing drivers.

Hardly had the race fans recovered from the excitement of that Whit Monday when they were back again for the Jaguar Drivers' Club meeting on June 13. This was the first race meeting organized by the JDC, a day mainly for the club driver. The chairman of the club wrote in the programme that he remembered the Palace before the war and was glad to be back at 'this lovely circuit'. The main race of the day was the Pontin Trophy for GT cars and featured the spectacular AC Cobras of Jack Sears and Frank Gardner, but many had come too to see the talked-about young

Scottish driver Jackie Stewart who drove the E-Type Jaguar of John Coombs.

The 'Bemsee' meeting of August 3, 1964, was expected to provide more wins for Joe Dunphy, but a poor grid position in the 125cc race meant he could get his Honda no higher than third. His miserable day continued in the 350cc race when he had clawed his Norton through to fifth but then the engine dropped a valve. His last race was for up-to-1,000cc bikes and he led on his 500cc Norton until the last lap, only to be beaten by the narrowest of margins across the line by the similar machine of John Simmonds. Very little is certain in motor sport!

Once again the BRSCC September meeting would close the season, kicking off with a Formula 3 race packed with aspiring young hopefuls looking for a way to the top. Among them were Piers Courage, driving a Lotus-Ford backed by the offshore pirate broadcasting station Radio Caroline, and New Zealander Howden Ganley driving a patriotically named Kiwi-Ford. However it was Chris Irwin in a Ginetta who won the race from pole position. The Anerley Trophy was run as a Formule Libre event for sports cars and single-seaters of unlimited capacity and despite the presence of some mighty cars like Roy Pierpoint's Attila-Ford and the Lotus-Chevrolet of Chris Summers, the

Peter Gethin driving Jack Playford's Lotus 23 in the Norbury Trophy race for sports-racing cars up to 1,150cc in September 1964.

J S Patterson was driving his Lola-Climax in the same race, but came unstuck and slid to a stop with smoke billowing from his rear tyres.

Race officials in the Shell control tower were provided with a commanding view of the startline area on the Terrace Straight, where a grid full of solos are seen here beginning the race at the August 1965 meeting.

smaller and more nimble Brabham-Climax of Frank Gardner won. The historic race went to Pat Lindsay's ERA Remus, and Jackie Oliver, more recently Arrows Grand Prix team boss, took GT honours in his Lotus Elan.

Easter Monday was late in 1965, falling on April 19, but no-one told the weather it should have been spring-like and a mixture of rain, snow and hail greeted a surprisingly large crowd at the Palace for the ACU season opener. Since the last meeting, the London County Council had become the Greater London Council, the boundaries of the capital being widened to take in some areas formerly under the jurisdiction of the county councils of Surrey, Kent, Middlesex and Essex. The new body agreed that racing should continue following its existing pattern, though the inevitable internal restructuring within the GLC brought various changes for the organizers.

On the track the change meant little and though speeds were kept down by the poor weather, the racing was close and competitive. By the mid-1960s, British bikes were beginning to be outclassed by foreign opposition, even for the club rider, so the 125cc race contained a proliferation of Honda and Bultaco machines. The larger classes were as yet mostly British-built, mainly Norton and AJS, but the odd 350 Yamaha was beginning to appear amongst the entry. The 250cc class was dominated by the Villiers-powered Greeves Silverstone, winner of the *Motor Cycle News* Machine of the Year award in 1964 and a very popular mount for the club racer. Its Essex-based constructors were of course more familiar for their trials and scrambles machines, but this was a neat, fast and very competitive road racing bike.

The first car races under the auspices of the new GLC were at the BRSCC International Meeting on Whit Monday, June 7, 1965. Formula 2 racing for the London Trophy topped the bill, with supporting races for sports, GT and saloon cars. Many of the top Grand Prix drivers of the day also competed in Formula 2 and the fine entry list confirmed this. The 1964 F2 champion, Jack Brabham, who had not raced at the Palace since 1957, was down to drive one of his own Brabhams powered by a 1-litre Honda engine, the Japanese firm just starting out on the road leading them to the dominant position in Formula 1 racing they enjoy today, but in fact both his car and that of team-mate Denny Hulme appeared with Cosworth-Ford engines this time. Also entered were Graham Hill in the John Coombs Brabham-BRM, three Ron Harris Team Lotus cars for Jim Clark, Peter Revson and Mike Spence, Chris Amon and Richard Attwood in Midland Racing Partnership Lola-Cosworths, Trevor Taylor in a Brabham, and the Roy

Paddock scenes at Crystal Palace before the start of racing on Whit Monday, 1965. Above left, a thoughtful Jochen Rindt returns to the scene where exactly a year before he had set the motor racing world alight with his stunning victory with his Formula 2 Brabham. Above, an animated Jim Clark about to set off in one of Ron Harris' works Lotus 35 Formula 2 cars. Left, an inquisitive Jack Brabham spots something interesting from the paddock while his driving partner Denny Hulme checks his helmet strap. Below left, a preoccupied John Surtees keeps warm on a chilly afternoon. Below, an amused Colin Chapman about to join Jim Clark in the victory parade to celebrate their recent history-making victory in the Indianapolis 500 in the United States.

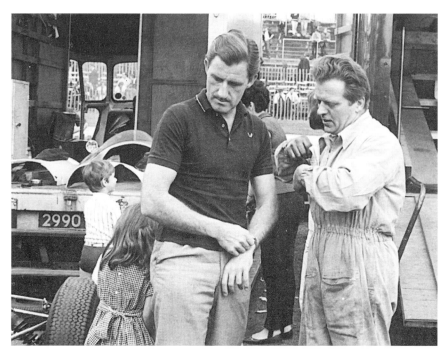

Above, Graham Hill and his race engineer check their watches during the build-up before the Formula 2 race as young Brigitte and Damon busy themselves in the background and try to keep out of Dad's way. Above right, motorhomes hadn't been thought of as essential paddock transport in 1965, and Jackie Stewart's changing room was the back seat of the Zodiac which the Ford Motor Company had loaned him. Right, Helen finds it amusing as a short-haired Jackie completes his quick-change act as modestly as conditions permit. Below, Graham Hill loved to tinker with his car, right up to within five minutes of the 'off' if necessary. Below right, Graham has a last look at the gear ratio chart, or is he sizing up the opposition in the race programme?

Winkelmann team Brabhams of those two Palace protagonists of the previous year, Alan Rees and Jochen Rindt. Palace fans could also welcome back another favourite, due to make his four-wheel debut on a track which 10 years earlier he had dominated on two wheels. John Surtees, who since those early days had taken seven 350cc and 500cc motorcycle world titles, and had become Formula 1 World Champion with Ferrari the previous season, completing a double unlikely to be equalled, was due to drive a Cooper-BRM for Ken Tyrrell's team. His team-mate, a young Scot at the beginning of a very fruitful partnership with the genial team boss, was Jackie Stewart.

The race was to be in two halves with an aggregate result, and Graham Hill took pole position for Part 1 with Clark and Stewart alongside. Rindt and Rees shared a rather lowly fourth row. Brabham made a flying start from row 3, too good as it earned him a 60-second penalty, and was third behind Clark and Stewart at the end of the first lap, with Mike Beckwith (Brabham) fourth and Hill fifth after a rather tardy start. Hill displaced Beckwith on lap 2 and the leading positions then held steady until lap 12 when Brabham took second from Stewart. Moving up through the field were Attwood, Rindt and Surtees. On lap 14 Hill took Brabham for third after Stewart had regained his second place, but the latter dropped out after another lap. Surtees was now up to fifth, but in front Jim Clark was in command and reeled off the last 10 laps to win from Graham Hill. Jack Brabham was third on the road but demoted by his penalty. John Surtees had looked a certain fourth but retired five laps from home, leaving Richard Attwood and Jochen Rindt third and fourth. The two 'Flying Scots', Clark and Stewart, set a new joint lap record at 55.8 seconds, 89.66mph.

The grid positions for Part 2 were determined by the results of the first half, but Jack Brabham preferred to take no further part in the proceedings because of his penalty and Peter Revson was excluded for receiving a push start. As before, it was Jim Clark who made all the running up front, dominating the race. Rindt initially followed him but was overtaken by Richard Attwood on lap 2. All eyes were on Graham Hill as he began to cut through the field, taking second place by lap 11. That's the way it finished, the overall results giving the London Trophy to Jim Clark, followed by Graham Hill, Richard Attwood and Jochen Rindt, with Rees fifth and Beckwith sixth.

The GT race had seen Boley Pittard in an Alfa Romeo GTZ dicing with Jackie Oliver's Lotus Elan, the latter getting the verdict, with the similar Elans of Eric Liddle and Malcolm Wayne third and fourth. Roy Pierpoint's 5-litre Mustang won the larger capacity saloon car race despite the efforts of a trio of three-wheeling Lotus Cortinas, the works cars of Jim Clark and Jack Sears plus Frank Gardner's Willment-entered example. Jim Clark set a new lap record during the pursuit. The smaller saloon category was by now Mini-Cooper territory, John Rhodes taking the Cooper Car entry to a win in a haze of tyre smoke. The Mini-Coopers of John Fitzpatrick (Broadspeed) and Gerry Marshall (NewTune) also featured in the results but Ford honour was upheld by Chris Craft's third-placed Anglia. The Elva Trophy for sports cars went to Denny Hulme's Brabham-Climax ahead of Tommy Hitchcock's similar car, with Chris Amon in Bruce McLaren's Elva-BMW third. Looking back, it's striking how the Grand Prix drivers of the day happily raced in the other formulae, too – so different from the sequestered stars of the 1980s and '90s!

Two more Saturdays that summer were set aside for car racing. July 3 saw the Jaguar Drivers' Club in charge, and July 31 was the BARC National Meeting at which the Bromley Bowl for Formula 3 cars was the main race and Chris Irwin's Brabham won heat and final. In the supporting races, Jackie Oliver (Lotus Elan) and Boley Pittard (Alfa GTZ), leading GT contenders at the previous meeting, had to settle for second and third as David Piper took the Norbury Trophy with his Ferrari 250LM.

Of course, not every event on the circuit was as fast and furious as these hotly contested races. For example, July 18 had seen the Veteran Car Club promoting one of many

Jack Brabham, already twice a World Champion, turned out at the wheel of the Alan Brown Racing Ford Mustang in the Norbury Trophy race for touring cars over 1,300cc at the 1965 Whit Monday meeting.

Jim Clark in characteristic pose, letting it all hang out as he explores the limit with his Ron Harris-managed Team Lotus 35.

World Champions all. Four years before his first title, Jackie Stewart, still learning his craft in Ken Tyrrell's Cooper-BRM, leading Graham Hill in John Coombs' Brabham-BRM and Jack Brabham in his works Brabham-Honda during the Formula 2 race in 1965. Between them, this talented trio would collect no fewer than eight World Championships between 1959 and 1973.

The reigning World Champion, John Surtees, then driving for Ferrari, switched to one of Ken Tyrrell's Cooper-BRMs for the Formula 2 race at Crystal Palace, the circuit on which in earlier years his star had shone so brightly on two wheels.

Solos streaming downhill through the New Link and the right-handed curve leading on to the former start-finish straight during the April 1966 meeting. With relatively narrow run-off areas before the vertical walls and barriers it was not the most comfortable place to drop a bike.

rallies at the track. These events typically consisted of a road run with cars starting from various points, converging on the finish and receiving marks for mileage covered and age of the vehicle. Once at the Palace there was usually a concours d'elegance with marks awarded for things like originality, cleanliness and presentation. There would be a series of driving tests including crossing imaginary ravines on plank bridges, treasure hunts, and various trials of manoeuvrability including driving through gates and between balloons without bursting them, following a route through the woods around the circuit, and even games like hoop-la and pontoon. Other clubs organized driving tests on the top straight, timed runs around various obstacle courses which often produced some fairly hairy motoring.

The final Palace meeting of 1965 was on August 30, Bank Holiday Monday, with 'Bemsee' in charge, and it was to be a day of record-breaking. Reg Everitt, riding his 250cc Yamaha, started the ball rolling when he broke Joe Dunphy's record, leaving it at 64.5 seconds (76.51mph), and also broke the race record which had been set by John Surtees in 1957. Then the Norton of John Blanchard took race and lap records for the 350cc class with a fastest lap at 64.6 seconds (77.46mph). Rounding off the day, Chris Williams broke his own vintage record on his 1926 Scott in

exactly 69 seconds, a speed of 72.52mph.

By the mid-1960s, Britain was, to many people, *the* place to be. Beatlemania was at its height, pirate radio and mini-skirts were in, the Mini was the in car. It was an exuberant, trendy and youthful culture, and it was a metropolitan one, too. Swinging London, and especially Carnaby Street, aspired to be the fashion capital of the world. Crystal Palace, playing its part in this explosion of leisure activities, with the Sports Centre now in full operation, was able to offer Londoners a whole variety of facilities. The Parks Department of the Greater London Council, based in County Hall on the banks of the Thames, was in charge of a range of amenities including not only the motor racing and athletics but also a children's zoo, fishing and boating lakes, play areas, a concert bowl, and there was still some very pleasant parkland remaining, too, complete with the famous concrete dinosaurs. With so many attractions confined to a relatively small site right in the heart of one of the most densely populated areas of the country, there was some delicate balancing of priorities to do: how long could things remain as they were?

Motor racing, though, seemed in a strong position. Britain not only led the world in pop music and fashion trends in the mid-1960s, but British motor sportsmen were hard to beat as well, with World Champions Jim Clark, Graham Hill and John Surtees as well as two-wheeler aces Mike Hailwood, Phil Read, Geoff Duke and Bill Ivy among their number. The Japanese invasion was making huge inroads on the bike scene but British cars dominated Grand Prix racing. Altogether, in 1966, interest in motor sport was generally high, helped by the advent of a new 3-litre Grand Prix formula. So the GLC were encouraged to push ahead with another season at the Palace in much the same format as usual.

On Easter Monday, April 11, the ACU were in charge, and it rained heavily. The bike racers had been in action on Good Friday at Brands Hatch and John Blanchard had taken a nasty tumble, but it did not dim his scintillating form and at the Palace he won both the 250cc and 350cc finals on Bultaco and Norton respectively. Martin Carney's Bultaco had been in the hunt for the smaller class, but he could not match Blanchard. Ron Chandler (Matchless) won the 500cc race and Rod Scivyer (Honda) the 125cc. Brian Hinckney's Triumph dominated the sidecar event.

On Whit Monday, May 30, the Formula 2 cars were back for the London Trophy meeting, a qualifying round for the *Autocar* Championship. First and second on the entry list and eventually first and second in the aggregate results were the green and gold Brabham-Hondas of Jack Brabham and Denny Hulme. For Brabham, 1966, the year he turned 40 and earned the nickname 'the old man of motor racing', was to prove extremely successful. Not only was he dominant in Formula 2, but the Ron Tauranac-designed 3-litre Repco-Brabham with its GM-based V8 engine took him to his third Formula 1 World Championship, the only time that a driver building his own cars had won the title. The following season his team-mate Hulme would be champion.

Jack's Palace win was one of 10 he took in Formula 2 that year, and Hulme won a further two, Jochen Rindt's Cosworth-powered Brabham providing the only real opposition to the Honda-engined works cars. The Japanese company made a huge effort to back the Brabham team, a large crew of mechanics working in the factory and turning out at each race, and technicians flying between England and Japan with engines and spares. Their dedication to success was well rewarded, for the reliability of the power unit was first rate and a Brabham car won every Formula 2 race started bar one. Brabham's championship wins received recognition at the end of the season when he was awarded the OBE. To his embarrassment, his road car proved less reliable than his racers, and next day's newspapers carried the story of how the motor racing World Champion, in best Moss Bros top hat and tails, came to have his head under the

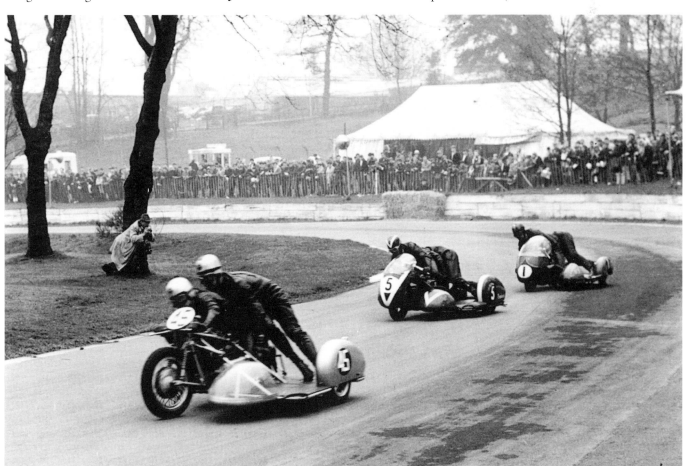

At the same meeting a photographer at North Tower Crescent has the psychological comfort of a stout tree as he aims his camera at a trio of combinations locked in battle on a drying track.

Bill McGovern, always spectacular at the wheel of Paul Emery's Hillman Imp, works hard to hold off the strong challenge of Anita Taylor's Broadspeed Ford Anglia in the 1,000cc saloon car race during the 1966 Whit Monday meeting.

Gordon Spice and his tyre-smoking Mini-Cooper S left Tony Lanfranchi taking a spin in his Mini in the 1,300cc saloon car race in the same programme.

More herocis by athletic sidecar passengers as they help their drivers speed uphill through Maxim Rise during the April 1965 meeting. The appearance of Armco alongside parts of the track was a sign of the changing times in motor sports, but was not all that enthusiastically received by the two and three-wheeled competitors.

bonnet of a car outside Buckingham Palace!

Back at the other Palace a few miles away, there had been a race for the remaining places behind the unbeatable Brabham-Hondas, and third and fourth went to the Winkelmann Racing Brabham-Cosworths of Alan Rees and Jochen Rindt. Chris Irwin, also driving a Brabham, had won the Formula 3 Bromley Bowl from Piers Courage (Lotus) and Peter Gethin in yet another Brabham. A very famous name appeared in a Lotus-Ford entered by Charles Lucas when Cacho Fangio, son of the five-times world champion, made his Crystal Palace debut. Supporting races for saloons had seen the usual Mini-Cooper versus Ford Anglia battles with John Rhodes and John Fitzpatrick starring, and a large Ford Falcon, veteran of Ford's Monte Carlo Rally effort, driven by Roy Pierpoint, defeated Jack Brabham driving Alan Brown's Mustang.

Most people were following the progress of the England football team on their way to the famous World Cup victory that summer, but the Palace racegoers still turned out on July 2 for the Holts Trophy meeting, around 8,000 of them arriving at the gates. Holts and Romac Car Care Products were a locally based company in the 1960s, with a head office in Croydon. The inaugural Holts Trophy race had been in September 1965 at Brands Hatch, but now the company moved a little closer home, and their support was rewarded by fine weather. Formula 3, with many up-and-coming young men, formed the main race and Peter Gethin (Brabham-Ford) won his heat and the Holts Trophy final, beating Harry Stiller, Chris Williams, David Cole and Mo Nunn across the line.

There were two meetings in the month of August, the BRSCC with cars on the 6th and 'Bemsee' back for the usual Bank Holiday thrash on August 29, which would also bring the curtain down on the 1966 season. The bikes entertained with fast and furious racing whilst the afternoon remained dry, but when the dark clouds overhead turned to rain the speeds fell, and so did some of the competitors. Trevor Barnes (Moto Guzzi) fought a spirited battle with Alan Peck

(Petty-Norton) to win the 350cc event. John Blanchard (Seely-Matchless) and Dave Chester (Norton) were fighting for the 500cc honours, but both subsequently retired leaving the American rider Lance Weil (Norton) to win. Reg Everitt's Yamaha had an easy win in the 250cc race and Chris Williams took his usual victory in the vintage race with his 1926 Scott.

1967 may be remembered as the year of flower-power and hippies, but at the Palace things were much the same as usual when the new season got under way with the Easter Monday ACU meeting on March 27. Ron Chandler won both the 350cc race on his AJS and the 500cc aboard his Matchless, rounding off a very successful Easter. On Good Friday he had raced to the 'King of Brands' title, and on Easter Sunday had finished second at Mallory Park. But at the latter meeting the motorcycle racing fraternity had been saddened by the death of Swiss sidecar ace Fritz Scheidegger in a crash at the hairpin on the Leicestershire circuit, so the atmosphere was gloomy at Crystal Palace the next day. Paul Smart took the 125cc race on his Honda, narrowly beating the similar machine of Rod Scivyer, but Smart was in turn pipped by Reg Everitt in the 250cc final. Mick Rowell took a good win in an exciting sidecar race.

The season's main Crystal Palace meeting, the Spring International on Whit Monday, May 29, was organized by the BRSCC and had attracted sponsorship from British United Airways. The BUA Trophy race for Formula 2 cars was to be run as two heats and a final and there was an excellent entry. The first heat was won by Jean-Pierre Beltoise in a Matra-Ford, the Matra company having French government backing in their bid for motor racing success. Second was John Surtees driving the works Lola, part of a long association with Eric Broadley's team, and Jack Oliver was third in a Lotus.

Heat 2 included, among others, Bruce McLaren in his own car, using Formula 2 races to keep his hand in while work progressed on his BRM-powered Grand Prix car, the New Zealander having followed his former Cooper team-mate Jack Brabham into the ranks of Formula 1 driver-constructors. Johnny Servoz-Gavin drove the second works Matra and a third Matra run by Ken Tyrrell Racing was in the hands of the young Belgian Jacky Ickx. Perhaps the most amazing entry was the front-engined U2-Ford of Arthur Mallock which demonstrated that a relatively uncomplicated design could still be competitive against the sophisticated racing machinery of the more affluent makers. Another interesting car was the Protos-Ford with its Frank Costin-designed wooden chassis and aircraft-style windscreen, two examples being run by Ron Harris Racing for drivers Brian Hart and Eric Offenstadt.

The crowd anticipated a thrilling final, for Jean-Pierre Beltoise was on pole position alongside Heat 2 winner Bruce McLaren and John Surtees, and they were not disappointed: Jacky Ickx in the Ken Tyrrell Matra came through from the third row to win. Ickx would underline his talent later that year in the German Grand Prix on the tortuous Nürburgring when Formula 2 cars were allowed to take part and his 1.6-litre Matra was running in fifth place ahead of many established names in their 3-litre Formula 1 cars. He took the European Formula 2 Championship in 1967 on his way to a career in Formula 1 and sports car racing which would include an as yet unequalled six wins at Le Mans. Jean-Pierre Beltoise came home second, completing a Matra 1–2, and in a subsequent interview for *Motor Racing* magazine he rated Crystal Palace amongst his favourite circuits. Bruce McLaren, for all his experience, could only manage third behind the 'new boys'. Prototype sports cars provided the supporting races with the Anerley Trophy going to Brian Redman's Chevron and the Norbury Trophy to the Ford GT40 of Paul Hawkins.

1967 marked 40 years since the first races on the paths round the Palace grounds and it was obvious that both the circuit and the sport had come on a long way since then, but the essential ingredient of man and machine matched against man and machine was still there, and the crowds still came to see the excitement. At the BARC meeting on August 5, Formula 3 was the principal attraction, the formula providing an ideal training ground for young hopefuls. So many aspiring young drivers entered that the race was run in two parts, the fastest man in practice getting pole position for race 'A', the second fastest pole for race 'B' and so on. Formula 3 drivers in the 1960s included Derek Bell, driving with Mac Daghorn and Peter Westbury in the Felday International team, Peter Gaydon, Tony Lanfranchi, Mike Beckwith, Mo Nunn, John Miles, Ian Ashley, Mike Walker, Tim Schenken, Chris Williams, Dave Walker, Gijs

John Britten considerably altered the shape of his MG Midget against one of Crystal Palace's unyielding walls when he needed more than the narrow run-off area during the Marque race in the August 1967 meeting. The medical man on the bank seems to be completely unperturbed by it all.

Jackie Oliver, later to direct the Shadow, Arrows and eventually Footwork Formula 1 teams, leads the works Coopers of Mike Beckwith and Peter Gethin through South Tower Corner in the Lotus Components type 41B during the BUA International Trophy race for Formula 2 cars in May 1967.

In the same event and on the same corner Jean-Pierre Beltoise manages to keep his Matra-Ford ahead of John Surtees' works Lola-Ford.

van Lennep and Tetsu Ikuzawa. The American driver Roy Pike won race 'A' in the Titan-Ford built by Charles Lucas and the same team's Brabham was second driven by Harry Stiller. Lucas himself rounded off a very successful day by winning race 'B' from Mo Nunn's Lotus and Peter Gethin's Brabham. Among the supporting races, saloons were particularly entertaining with Camaros, Falcons and Mustangs pitted against some examples of a newly emerging breed of highly modified cars including a 5½-litre Chevrolet-powered Viva and a V8-engined Cortina.

On August Bank Holiday Monday, 'Bemsee' were back for the usual second motorcycle meeting and a fortnight later the Holts Trophy race was run once again at Crystal Palace, the sponsors obviously pleased with the amount of local interest shown. Managing Director Michael Holt wrote in the programme of his enthusiasm and support for motor racing, expressing his view that the motor industry as a whole owed a debt to the sport. Adding variety to the racing at this meeting was a 'Cavalcade of Speed' which featured many of the cars raced at the Palace before the war, and some driving tests in and out of marker cones along the top straight in which Midgets and Sprites took part, as well as some specials, all handled with great skill. Alan Allard and Tony Densham also demonstrated their dragsters: Allard then held the world

record for the standing-start quarter-mile at 9.33 seconds (over 170mph) and Densham had a new 7-litre machine called 'The Commuter'. The cars were run singly, starting at South Tower, and reached 130mph in about 5 seconds before having to use their parachutes to slow down – negotiating North Tower in a dragster could prove rather tricky! It was a first taste of this impressive spectacle for a lot of the crowd and no doubt encouraged many to visit drag racing venues and see more of this sport, new to Britain.

Racing 'proper' included the first Formula Vee race to be held at the Palace. This was a new formula for simple single-seaters using the familiar air-cooled VW engine as well as the gearbox and suspension components of the Beetle. Nick Brittan (Beach Vee) was the winner. The Holts Trophy itself was for the larger capacity sports-racers competing for points in the *Motoring News* GT Championship. The big Lola T70-Chevrolets of Frank Gardner and Mike de Udy finished first and second. David Piper had the misfortune to spin his Ferrari P2 at South Tower after fading brakes caused him problems, his beautiful car suffering minor damage. Michael Holt's wife presented Gardner with his trophy to the applause of 10,000 spectators. Harry Stiller won the Formula 3 race from Derek Bell, both driving Brabhams, and another GT race (won by John Miles in a

Once again on top form, Jochen Rindt, driving a Roy Winkelmann Brabham BT23C, leading a tightly bunched Jackie Oliver (Lotus 48), Henri Pescarolo (Matra MS7), Jacky Ickx (Ferrari Dino 166) and Peter Gethin (Chevron B9) in the Formula 2 Holts Trophy race in June 1968.

Brian Redman needs an armful of opposite-lock to keep David Bridges' Lola T100 pointing the right way during the Holts Trophy race.

Right, Jacky Ickx indulges in a spot of grass cutting with his Ferrari Dino as Jackie Oliver's Lotus 48 and Piers Courage's Frank Williams-entered Brabham BT23C follow a more conventional line through South Tower Corner.

Lotus 47) and two saloon car events further enlivened the proceedings. A local newspaper, *The Croydon Midweek*, had put up a trophy for the historic car race, and it was little surprise when the celebrated ERA Remus took the Hon Patrick Lindsay to another fine win.

Another season at the Palace closed: how many more would there be? The next, 1968, would see a novel one-off event later in the year, but it began in the time-honoured way at Easter with the ACU meeting, just a little unusual in that the first race was the sidecar event which the experienced Mick Rowell (Honda) won from Gerry Boret (Vincent). The motor racing world was still reeling from the shock of Jim Clark's death a week before Easter. It seemed incredible that the Scot, twice World Champion, winner of Indianapolis and, at that time, winner of more Grands Prix than anyone else, could perish in a racing accident, particularly in a relatively unimportant Formula 2 event at Hockenheim.

So it was a much saddened Formula 2 fraternity that met at Crystal Palace for the Spring International Holts Trophy meeting on Whit Monday, June 3. The race was the fourth in the 1968 European Formula 2 Championship and the current leader was Jean-Pierre Beltoise who led his fellow countryman and Matra team-mate Henri Pescarolo by 17 points. Only 'non-graded' drivers, the less experienced

among the up-and-coming men, were eligible for the championship, though 'graded' drivers, who were previous champions or Grand Prix pilots, could compete for individual wins. Four of the latter were at the Palace. There was Jacky Ickx, reigning F2 champion and winner at the Palace the previous year, a member of the Ferrari team, driving the lone works Dino 166, a gorgeous little car just like a miniature Formula 1 machine. Jochen Rindt, needing no introduction to Palace racegoers, was once again in a Roy Winkelmann Brabham-Cosworth, and Pedro Rodriguez, the fiery little Mexican, a member of the BRM Grand Prix team, was driving a Tecno for Ron Harris racing. The fourth graded driver present was Graham Hill, in the works team Lotus-Cosworth – Colin Chapman's team had but one car at Crystal Palace, not the two which had been expected before the Hockenheim tragedy. For 1968, Team Lotus were receiving sponsorship from the John Player tobacco company and in place of the familiar British Racing Green and yellow livery, the cars were now painted red, white and gold like a Gold Leaf cigarette packet, complete with the sailor's head on the cockpit side. This was the first time that sponsorship had been so loudly proclaimed on a car racing in Europe and it marked the end of the convention of national racing colour schemes, reflecting both the increasingly multinational nature of the sport and the rapidly rising cost which made major sponsorship more and more essential.

Amongst the ungraded entry were Piers Courage, driving a Brabham for Frank Williams, Derek Bell in the Church Farm Racing Brabham, Jack Oliver in the Herts and Essex Aero Club Lotus, Henri Pescarolo in one works Matra and Johnny Servoz-Gavin, standing in for the absent Beltoise, in the other. Frank Gardner had the Chequered Flag McLaren M4A, Peter Gethin drove a Chevron, Max Mosley had the second Frank Williams car, Alan Rees the other Winkelmann entry, Brian Redman had a Lola and Clay Regazzoni the works Tecno.

Two heats and a final were needed to sort it all out, and intermittent rain caused problems for competitors and spectators alike. The first eight in each heat would qualify for the final. Ickx, Rindt and Oliver started from the front row of Heat 1 and the Austrian took an immediate lead with Oliver, Pescarolo and Ickx in pursuit. The Ferrari driver quickly began to move up, taking third place on lap 3 and second a lap later. A few places down the field, Courage and Bell were making up ground. On lap 7 Ickx had a moment which cost him six places and Courage moved up, disputing third place with Oliver. Derek Bell too was challenging strongly. By half-distance Rindt still led but Courage had

taken Pescarolo, with Bell, Oliver, Chris Lambert, Frank Gardner and Ickx racing hard behind. With two laps to go Pescarolo retook Courage for second place, but this was short-lived, the Frenchman dropping out a lap later. At the flag Rindt was a clear winner, the other seven qualifiers being Courage, Bell, Oliver, Ickx, Lambert, Attwood and Gardner. Breathless racing – and this was just the first heat! Rindt set the fastest lap at 96.6mph, the 100mph lap getting closer though still just out of reach.

For Heat 2 Brian Redman (Lola) was on pole with Kurt Ahrens and Pedro Rodriguez alongside. Ahrens led away and behind him the race quickly settled into a fairly orderly procession with the first four places unchanging throughout. The first eight at the finish were Ahrens, Redman, Regazzoni, Robin Widdows, Rodriguez, Servoz-Gavin, Jo Schlesser and Graham Hill.

Before the final, two saloon car races kept the crowd entertained, the smaller capacity class providing a Mini-Cooper 1-2-3 with Steve Neal first from John Handley and John Rhodes. In the larger class, Brian Muir in Bill Shaw's Ford Falcon just beat the then brand new Twin Cam Escort of the Alan Mann Racing Team, driven by Frank Gardner.

Perhaps unsurprisingly, Jochen Rindt led from flag to flag in the 90-lap final, but behind him there were many

battles and incidents. Ickx and Rodriguez failed to complete the first lap, crashing out together to leave Ahrens and Courage dicing for second place. The Englishman took the German on lap 8, but Ahrens hung on, trying so hard that two laps later he overdid it and he too was out. Redman, Regazzoni, Bell and Oliver filled the next places and things settled down for a few laps. At the back, Graham Hill was having a difficult time and although he picked up places slowly his race would end when he lost a wheel at Maxim Rise. At half-distance another leading runner disappeared as Derek Bell crashed out of his comfortable fourth place. Then on lap 65 Piers Courage retired from his unchallenged second place and it seemed to be all over. On lap 71 Schlesser took his McLaren past Jack Oliver's Lotus, but the Frenchman was to crash on the penultimate lap, eventually being classified fifth. Jochen Rindt scored a hugely popular win with an equally impressive Brian Redman some 30 seconds behind, Regazzoni third and Oliver fourth. Graham Hill's troubled day would soon be forgotten as his Grand Prix exploits took him to a closely fought World Championship and dispelled some of the gloom cast over Team Lotus by Clark's death.

Multi-coloured advertising decorating the bodywork of racing cars was not the only striking innovation to be seen on the circuits in 1968. In search of a 'something-for-nothing' increase in grip and cornering power, Formula 1 designers began experimenting with aerofoils mounted on spindly looking struts high above the car, following a trend started in 1966 when Jim Hall's Chaparral sports-racers used them in CanAm racing and in some European endurance events. During the season many variations on the idea appeared, but it was quickly discovered that while lap speeds could be greatly increased, some of the effects were difficult to predict and, in particular, structural failure of the wing supports could cause complete loss of control as downforce turned to lift. Following some bad accidents including one involving both Team Lotus cars at the 1969 Spanish Grand Prix, in which Jochen Rindt broke his jaw and nose, all high-

mounted and movable aerodynamic devices were banned. Fixed wings, at body level, though, were to be an important feature of all subsequent Formula 1 designs.

All this high technology took longer to filter through to the lower echelons of the sport, however, and most of the Formula 3 cars at the next Palace meeting, on August 3, 1968, were still unadorned by wings or spoilers. Roy Pike, subject of the 'Palace Portrait' in the programme, led the race all the way, winning the Anerley Trophy, in his Titan-Ford. Second was Chris Craft (Tecno), at that time better known as a saloon racer in his Anglia, third was the Chevron of Tim Schenken, and fourth was Pike's team-mate and constructor of the Titan, Charles Lucas. The other single-seater race featured a brand new category, Formula Ford, brainchild of John Webb and Motor Racing Stables at Brands Hatch (encouraged by the Ford Motor Company). The formula was in its infancy in 1968 and few, perhaps, could foresee the impact it would have over the next 20 years as it became the most successful way in for newcomers to the sport and the first rung on the ladder to Grand Prix racing. Tony Trimmer won the first Formula Ford race at Crystal Palace, driving a Brabham for the fledgling Frank Williams team. Behind him came Australian Dave Walker in an Alexis, entered by the Jim Russell Racing Drivers' School, its founder well known for his Palace exploits of the previous decade.

Races for sports cars, GTs and saloons completed the afternoon's events. The beautiful Ferrari Dino 206S won the smaller capacity GT race in the hands of Tony Dean, whilst Ed Nelson took the larger class in his Ford GT40. The other sports winner was John Bridges in the Red Rose Motors Chevron, and the two saloon races were both victories for Mini-Coopers, the drivers being Harry Ratcliffe (in the smaller class) and Ian Mitchell, both cars proving more nimble round the twists and turns of the Palace track than more powerful adversaries.

A month later and there was more two-wheeled action at the usual 'Bemsee' date, with 13 races and plenty of trophies

Rain, which had been threatening earlier in the meeting, finally arrived to spoil the final of the 1968 Holts Trophy race. Here, the spray from Graham Hill's Lotus 48 makes life difficult for Robin Widdows in the Chequered Flag-entered McLaren M4A and Alan Rees in the Winkelmann Brabham BT23C.

Frank Gardner avoids the puddles in his Alan Mann-entered Ford Escort Twin Cam as he holds off David Hobbs, at the wheel of Malcolm Gartlan's Ford Falcon, in a 1968 British Saloon Car Championship race for over-2,000cc cars.

It rained again for the September 1968 meeting while Tony Dean kept his Ferrari Dino 206 ahead of Derek Bennett's Chevron B6 and Chris Skeeping's Chevron B8 in the Holts Trophy race for Special GT cars.

up for grabs. Members of the Morgan Three Wheeler Club took part in a demonstration race with a collection of classic machinery. Star of the afternoon was Ray Pickrell, a 30-year-old printer from Harrow who had never raced at the Palace despite his seven years in motorcycle racing which included a win in the Production TT on the Isle of Man the previous June. Overcoming his lack of familiarity with the track, he was successful in the Production race on his 745cc Dunstall and also won the final round of the Players No 6 Championship from Ron Chandler (Matchless) and the eventual champion Malcolm Uphill (Norton). The 350cc race proved the most hard-fought with five different leaders in the 10 laps. Initially, Terry Grotefield's Yamaha led the pack for two laps before Martyn Ashwood (AJS) took over. A lap later the Kawasaki of Rex Butcher was in front but he had the Moto Guzzi ridden by John Blanchard hard on his heels and it took the lead a lap later. On the seventh tour, Ron Chandler (AJS) took over at the front and, despite immense pressure from Butcher, managed to hold out to the flag, with Ashwood third, Chris Singleton (Aermacchi) fourth and Paul Smart (Ducati) fifth, barely a second behind the winner.

Another Holts Trophy meeting, continuing the company's successful association with motor racing, came next, on September 14, organized as ever by the BARC. There were a number of championship rounds as well as driving tests on the top straight and a demonstration run by 'Chitty Chitty Bang Bang', one of several cars built by Alan Mann Racing for the making of a musical film of the same name (and not, of course, Count Zborowski's legendary aero-engined Brooklands racer of the 1920s, with which the film's only connection was the borrowed title). The imitation antique was driven by Jenny Nadin, who also drove in the Formula Vee race.

During the morning practice, the rain was pouring down, and this doubtless meant that many people decided to stay at home, but by the time the flag fell on event three the skies had cleared and the sunshine quickly dried the track, making for a pleasant afternoon's racing. The Holts Trophy this time was a 20-lap race for Special GT cars and once more Tony Dean's very pretty Dino 206S proved unbeatable, beating the Chevron-BMW of Derek Bennett by an enormous margin. The over-1,000cc saloon race saw a tremendous tussle between Roger Taylor's Escort Twin Cam and the 1,275cc Mini-Cooper S of John Handley. Two-tenths of a second had separated them in practice and so closely matched were they that there was the same margin between them at the chequered flag. In the race for smaller capacity saloons a nasty accident befell pole-position man Keith Holland when he lost his Alan Fraser Imp at the Glade on the opening lap, the resultant collision with a tree badly damaging the car: the driver was taken to hospital, fortunately without serious injury. Bill McGovern's Imp overcame the Mini of Peter Wilcox to win. Richard Lloyd (Triumph Spitfire) and John Lewis (Jaguar E-Type) had taken sports car race wins, and Gerry Birrell (Austro-Vee) won the Formula Vee event. The meeting was rounded off by John Miles who took the Gold Leaf Team Lotus 47 Europa look-alike to an easy win in the second Special GT race.

That was it for the season as far as regular race meetings were concerned, but the location of Crystal Palace in the capital made it the ideal choice for another, one-off motoring event. On November 24, 1968, the circuit was host to the start of the London to Sydney Marathon. Enormous popular interest was aroused by the publicity for this great motoring extravaganza, and the vast crowd that arrived at the Palace was by far the largest ever seen there.

The Marathon was the brainchild of Jocelyn Stevens, Tommy Sopwith and Sir Max Aitken and it was sponsored by the *Daily Express* and the *Sydney Telegraph*. There was a £10,000 first prize and the original plan was for a distance of 10,000 miles to be covered in 10 days. After a mammoth job of organization, the route chosen would lead the competitors from Crystal Palace into central London, then via Dover and Calais to Paris, down to Turin, across Yugoslavia to Belgrade, and then on through Turkey, Persia, Afghanistan, Pakistan and India to Bombay. From Bombay there was a sea crossing to Fremantle followed by a gruelling trek across the Australian desert and up through the Snowy Mountains before arriving in Sydney on December 17. It was a motoring adventure on an unprecedented scale and it attracted a large and diverse entry, experienced rally crews, with varying degrees of factory support, competing alongside ambitious amateurs drawn by the romance of the project. The cars to be used, some of them highly modified, were equally diverse, representing most of the major manufacturers but also including some most unusual choices like a 1930 Bentley.

A total of 98 cars actually started, and their departure from Crystal Palace was accompanied by suitable celebrations, the entertainment including demonstration laps by World Champion Graham Hill in a Lotus 49. He drove the 'Chitty Chitty Bang Bang' film car, too, and there was a parade of historic competition cars representing the whole history of rallying. A fanfare from the Royal Marines sent the first of the competitors on their way, the first hazard they were to encounter being the huge traffic jams in the crowded streets of South London.

Far greater hazards were to follow, though. There were countless mishaps and adventures and some amazing feats of endurance. It is now history that the Hillman Hunter of Andrew Cowan, Brian Coyle and Colin Malkin scored a plucky and somewhat unexpected victory. Just finishing was in itself a major achievement, and 56 of the original 98 starters arrived in Sydney. It had been a long drive from Crystal Palace!

Spring returned to South London as the ACU got the 1969 season under way, as always on Easter Monday, April 7. It was to be a record-breaking day, beginning when John Ringwood set new lap and race records on his 125cc MZ while beating a young Barry Sheene (Bultaco) and Charles Mortimer's similar machine. He repeated this feat with a win in the 250cc race on his Yamaha. A three-way scrap enlivened the 350cc race as Ray Pickrell (Aermacchi), Paul Smart (Ducati) and Mick Andrew (Kuhn Seeley) diced for the lead, Andrew eventually winning with a flying final lap which broke another record. Then Ray Pickrell took a comfortable win and another lap record on his 745cc Dunstall in the 1,000cc race. Yet more records were set in the sidecar final as Chris Vincent and Peter Brown, both on 650 BSA outfits, thrilled the crowd. At half-distance Brown

From time to time Crystal Palace was the scene of a gentler type of two-wheeled activity when it hosted a vintage motorcycle rally and assembled the competitors on the early part of the Terrace Straight, immediately after South Tower Corner. This picture was taken during the 1966 event.

pulled out a lead as Vincent's machine began to misfire, but by lap 8 the engine cleared and Vincent put on a masterly show, just beating his opponent to the line.

At the Whit Monday BRSCC International Meeting on May 26, 1969, the hitherto regular Formula 2 race was replaced by a Formula 3 event, and though the drivers were mostly 'coming men' as distinct from the established names in Formula 2, the entry list was very good and the closely matched 1-litre 'screamers' provided excellent sport on the twisty track. Many of the drivers would have places in Formula 1 within a season or two and most had something to prove. Heat 1 saw Tim Schenken in Rodney Bloor's Sports Motors Manchester Brabham-Ford win from Roy Pike in the Gold Leaf Team Lotus-Ford. Tetsu Ikuzawa brought his Mike Spence-entered Lotus home third, and the amazing EMC-Ford built by Dr Jo Erlich gave Briton Roger Keele fourth place. Formula 3 was certainly an international affair! On lap 1 the Swedish driver Lief Hallgren (Merlyn) had tried the aerial approach to North Tower Crescent as wheels became entangled, and crashed down on top of the sleepers, scattering the marshals and scaring the spectators.

Heat 2 was won by Peter Hanson's Chevron from Peter Gaydon in a Tecno. In the third heat, two rising Swedish stars finished second and third as the Tecno of Ronnie Peterson and the Chevron of Reine Wisell were beaten to

the line by Alan Rollinson's Brabham. Amongst all this talented competition, the bright red works-supported Brabham-Ford of Tim Schenken came out a well-deserved winner in the final.

In the supporting saloon car races there were wins for Frank Gardner's Alan Mann Escort and for Gordon Spice in the Britax-Cooper-Downton Mini-Cooper, the latter beating Vince Woodman in an Escort GT. The Brian Lister Trophy Race for historic sports cars was led from start to finish, not inappropriately, by the Lister-Jaguar of David Beckett, with Brian Groot's Allard in second place.

Formula 3 seemed to guarantee exciting races and topped the bill again for the BARC *Daily Express* Trophy Meeting on August 2. This time Reine Wisell took pole position in the works Chevron, joined on the front row by Roy Pike's Gold Leaf Lotus and Tim Schenken in the Brabham. Mike Beuttler, Bev Bond, Alan Rollinson and Mike Beckwith were amongst those behind them. Wisell was in top form, and, despite the efforts of Schenken to repeat his earlier win, took the chequered flag, with Roy Pike third. A 10-lap Formula Vee race went to Steve Matchett's Austro-Vee, racing driver and deep-sea diver Fred Saunders enlivening proceedings by repeating the air display at North Tower!

The *Motoring News* GT race was won from the second row by David Prophet's McLaren M6 GT. This extremely pretty car was a closed sports-racer developed from the M6 which

99

New Zealander Howden Ganley at the wheel of his Formula 3 Chevron-Ford for the Greater London Trophy race on Whit Monday in 1969.

The influence of wedge-shaped aerodynamics behind the cockpit is evident in this view, from the same spot, of Mike Beckwith's Formula 3 Lotus 59.

had dominated the North American CanAm series. It had been intended for endurance racing but homologation problems had ruled that out, although four were eventually constructed, one being used as a road car by Bruce McLaren himself. An older McLaren, a Ford-powered M3B driven by Alistair Cowin, gave Prophet a few problems and finished second. Another good-looking car, proving successful in the smaller-capacity GT race, was Roger Nathan's Frank Costin-designed Astra, racing for the first time with a Cosworth FVA engine replacing the ageing Coventry Climax unit.

Monday, September 1 saw the Palace hosting the final rounds of the 350cc and 500cc motorcycle road racing championships, the racing proving close and spectacular, and not short of incidents either. The 350cc championship was being led by Derek Chatterton but he was unable to defend his lead at this meeting as he was racing at Cadwell Park. When Mick Andrew took a nasty tumble at Ramp Bend in the production event and consequently withdrew from the 350cc race, his Seeley was available for Pat Mahoney instead of his regular bike to take fourth place which was enough to secure his first national title. In front of Mahoney, the race had seen a scrap between Graham Sharp (Aermacchi) and the Seeley machines of Dave Croxford, John Blanchard and Ron Chandler. With BBC

Grandstand viewers enjoying the action, drama occurred at South Tower when Croxford hit a patch of oil and crashed from his machine, and Blanchard damaged his bike avoiding the fallen rider. This left Chandler in a comfortable lead, and the AJS of Charlie Sandby took second, whilst Pat Mahoney and Graham Sharp disputed third place all the way to the flag. Ron Chandler also rode a Seeley to a win in the 500cc round after an exciting struggle with the Francis Seeley of Paul Smart, but third place for Dave Croxford was enough to secure his championship title. In the final 1,000cc race, Charlie Sandby set a new outright lap record for two-wheelers at 61.6 seconds, 81.23mph, before crashing off his 750 Kuhn Commando at South Tower Corner.

To round off the racing season at the Palace in 1969, the BARC organized the British Road Services Trophy Meeting on September 13, and once again BBC TV cameras were there to broadcast the event for *Grandstand*. The BRS Trophy race itself was run in two 20-lap parts for GT cars. Pole position was taken by Roger Nathan's Astra, the little 1,600cc racer once again proving quickest at the Palace despite much larger opposition, including two cars of David Prophet's, his McLaren M6, now clad in open CanAm type bodywork, which he was to drive himself, and a Lola T70 coupe to be handled by Alistair Cowin, another T70 for Max

Wilson, and John Wilson in Cowin's older McLaren sports car. Tony Lanfranchi had Mark Konig's Mk2 Nomad-BRM on the front row, too, and as the flag fell he took off into the lead, despite having had difficulties getting the engine to fire before the start. Behind him, Nathan kept the larger cars at bay before he squeezed the Astra into the lead on lap 3 and was never headed again. Lanfranchi was then involved in a battle with John Wilson who tried to outbrake the Nomad at North Tower on lap 12: the two cars touched, the McLaren spinning and restarting in eighth position. This had allowed both Prophet's McLaren and Cowin's Lola past Lanfranchi, and they began to close on Nathan. But Prophet's challenge evaporated in a cloud of steam and oil smoke when his engine expired, so Nathan was able to ease off and cruise home. Part 2 began with the Astra once again leading from pole position after Lanfranchi was left on the grid with a dead engine. Chris Skeaping held onto second place until lap 4 when he stopped at Park Curve with flames licking the back of the car, the result of a ruptured fuel line, and the fire marshals doused car and driver with foam. Cowin and Max Wilson now filled second and third places, and behind them Tony Lanfranchi was cutting through the field like a knife through butter after his start-line delay, although he had a 1-minute penalty for a push start to make up for. When the engine note of the Astra began to falter, it looked as if the battling trio behind might catch the leader, but Nathan was not to be beaten and came out a worthy winner from Alistair Cowin (McLaren) with the Nomad gaining third place overall.

The Formula 3 race, over two heats and a final, was for the Reg Parnell Trophy, presented to the BARC by Parnell's widow Betty in his memory and previously raced for at Goodwood, the Sussex circuit which had closed for racing three years earlier. For Heat 1 Charles Lucas had pole position in his Titan, alongside Harry Stiller's works Merlyn and the Gold Leaf Team Lotus entry of Roy Pike. They kept this order for a couple of laps before the American driver in the Lotus passed Stiller and then set about Lucas, taking him at North Tower on lap 8 to win. Behind those two, Bev Bond in the other Gold Leaf car finished third. Heat 2 had Howden Ganley on pole and beside him, racing at the Palace for the first time, was a sensational young Brazilian driver who had only come to Britain that summer and was already taking the motor racing world by storm. Emerson Fittipaldi had raced motorbikes, karts and saloons in Brazil with his older brother Wilson, and had cleaned up in Formula Ford since arriving in England. Into Formula 3, driving a green Lotus 59 for the Jim Russell Drivers' School, he was soon dominating the Lombank

Australian Tim Schenken exiting North Tower Crescent with the Sports Motors (Manchester) Formula 3 Brabham-Ford during the 1969 Greater London Trophy race.

Championship. His meteoric rise would continue with a Grand Prix debut in 1970 at Brands Hatch and a win in the USA GP that year, followed by two World Championships, in 1972 and 1974, and great success in American CART racing more recently. At the Palace in 1969, however, most people had barely heard of him and were amazed as he shot from the centre of the front row to lead the field. Howden Ganley, whose Chevron had a new Lucas engine installed, hung on and took the lead on the approach to Ramp Bend but Fittipaldi was soon ahead again. Behind them, Richard Scott, Mo Nunn, Tony Trimmer and James Hunt enjoyed a spirited dice. On lap 7, Ganley left his braking for Ramp very late and took Fittipaldi once more, finally crossing the line in the lead by just four-tenths of a second. As the finalists lined up for the 15-lap decider, Roy Pike, Charles Lucas and Howden Ganley formed the front row, with Emerson Fittipaldi and Richard Scott on row 2. Lucas was first away, with Ganley, Pike and Fittipaldi in pursuit, the Brazilian taking third on the lower straight. Scott and Bev Bond joined the leading group, the six cars pulling away

from the pack. By half-distance, Fittipaldi had taken over the lead from Lucas, Ganley and Pike. Behind them, Richard Scott had lost fifth place to the Lotus of Mo Nunn. Lucas regained the lead for two more laps before it changed hands for the final time as Fittipaldi took over once more. Lap 13 proved unlucky for Ganley as he tried to take Lucas at Ramp Bend and spun down into sixth place, slowing Lucas and Pike a little and allowing the young Brazilian to romp home to his most important win to date. Again, Formula 3 had been a real crowd-pleaser, and it was clear that Emerson Fittipaldi was on his way to the top of the motor racing ladder.

So the season and the decade came to a close at Crystal Palace. The 10 years had seen a great deal of change, for not only had the venue been transformed by the arrival of the sports centre but motor racing too had altered, becoming far more professional, the impact of both sponsorship and rapid technical development producing a far-reaching shift in standards and attitudes. Things would continue to change rapidly, and perhaps not always for the better.

The talented Swede Ronnie Peterson was always a joy to watch in a racing car. Here he tackles North Tower Crescent in the Tecno supported by Vick Scandinavia for the Greater London Trophy race.

CHAPTER 7

Crystal Palace on borrowed time

Motor racing's concluding years, 1970 to 1972

The changes in the world of motor sport were very evident as the new decade opened. Large-budget advertising was setting the style in international events and the days of the private entrant in anything above club level were numbered. The cars and bikes were enveloped in major sponsors' colour schemes and logos, and peppered with the decals of secondary backers and component suppliers. Glamorous promotion girls appeared at meetings offering the racegoer samples of anything from cigarettes to after-shave.

Behind the razzmatazz there were other changes, too. The question of safety was receiving much more attention than before, partly as a result of a number of recent fatalities: circuit owners and organizers were being required to do much more to protect competitors and spectators alike, and the ever rising speeds achieved by increasingly sophisticated racing machinery made the task an ever more demanding one. The Grand Prix Drivers' Association, under the leadership of Jackie Stewart, called for the installation of many more safety fences and crash barriers and the removal of hazards like earth banks and trees that were too close to the track. Crystal Palace obviously could not escape the attention of the drivers, particularly as it hosted an international meeting in May, and any safety measures incorporated for the professional competitors would benefit the clubmen as well. But it was all going to cost a great deal of money. The Palace had almost always run at a loss, and despite vigorous promotion – adverts in local, national and specialist motoring publications, and posters in main-line and underground railway stations as well as in all the other London parks – crowds at most meetings were becoming smaller. The GLC had a limited budget for leisure amenities and as the demand for money for safety measures at the circuit grew, so did the feeling in the GLC hierarchy that perhaps motor sport at the Palace was coming to the end of the line.

The drivers had inspected the circuit and their representative Francois Cevert, Tyrrell Grand Prix driver and team-mate to Jackie Stewart, felt that an Armco barrier should be erected on the inside of North Tower Crescent. The management did not relish the idea of a steel structure so close to the Concert Bowl, and nobody could recall a car crashing off on the inside of that corner anyway. Cevert suggested a demountable barrier, but when it was discovered that the cost of this and other safety measures would be about £250,000 there were very long faces at the GLC.

However, the season began in the time-honoured fashion on Easter Monday with the Metropolitan Meeting organized by the ACU. Eight riders disputed the lead in the 1,000cc race, the win eventually going to Charlie Sandby (750 Kuhn Seeley) from Martin Carney's Kawasaki. A gaggle of riders behind them swapped places throughout the race, the final order being Paul Smart (Norton), Graham Sharp (Kuhn Seeley), Rex Butcher (Yamaha), Martin Ashwood (Rickman Metisse), Alan Barnett (Seeley) and Charlie Brown (Norton). Many of the other races had close finishes, Charles Mortimer (250 Broad Yamaha) taking a narrow win over Paul Smart. The weather was as cold as the racing was hot, and Chris Williams rode his 1926 Scott to a vintage race win to close the proceedings.

The BARC were in charge for the International Trophy Formula 2 Race, sponsored in 1970 by Alcoa, the Aluminium Company of America. Practice took place on Saturday, May 23, with the race on Monday, and many competitors took a trip to Zolder in Belgium on the Sunday to fit in another Formula 2 race. Jochen Rindt was the winner there, his Lotus leading Derek Bell's Brabham across the line.

Back in London, the entry list contained not only Rindt and Bell but also 1969 World Champion Jackie Stewart driving the John Coombs Brabham BT30, Graham Hill and Emerson Fittipaldi (Lotus), Carlos Reutemann and John Watson (Brabham), Reine Wisell (Chevron), Ronnie Peterson (March) and the works Tecnos of Francois Cevert and Clay Regazzoni who had their own private practice session owing to the late arrival of their transporter at the circuit.

Stewart won the first heat from Cevert's Tecno with Reutemann third and Hill fourth, while Rindt took the

Jochen Rindt, for whom Crystal Palace regulars held a special affection after his sensational debut at the circuit in 1964, paid his final visit in 1970, a few months before his tragic death while practising for the Italian Grand Prix towards the end of a season which would make him motor racing's only posthumous World Champion.

honours in Heat 2 from Regazzoni, Andrea de Adamich (Brabham) and Fittipaldi. The final was another Palace thriller. Rindt led the field into North Tower from Regazzoni and Stewart. As Rindt pulled slowly away from his pursuers, Stewart was trying all he knew to find a way past Regazzoni, shaking his fist in frustration at the Tecno driver's tactics. After 22 laps he succeeded in passing and set off after Rindt who had a 4-second lead. Unfortunately the chase was short-lived for two laps later a disappointed Rindt coasted to a halt at the Glade with a broken battery lead. This left Stewart to win by just over 12 seconds from the charging Regazzoni, with Fittipaldi third, de Adamich fourth, Hill fifth and Henri Pescarolo (Brabham) sixth. Rindt's consolation was that during his heat he had become the first driver to lap Crystal Palace at over 100mph, and the GLC had a handsome silver plate made to be presented to him. Alas, he was never to see this prize, and the Palace fans were never again to see this driver who had first come to prominence on the circuit. Four months later, Jochen was killed at Monza in his Gold Leaf Team Lotus 72. The plate had by then been engraved for him, and so it fell to circuit manager Allan Tyler to present it to Rindt's widow Nina.

The spectators that Spring Holiday might have had a different kind of superstar to cheer from the Crystal Palace terraces. The motor racing feature film *Winning* had just opened at London cinemas and its star Paul Newman, a racing driver in his own right, had offered to come to England to race and promote the picture. But he wanted £25,000 appearance money and the GLC did not think it prudent to spend such an amount, despite the assurances of circuit manager Tyler that Newman's presence would double the gate. Nevertheless, some 25,000 people lined the track that day. Apart from Stewart's win, they saw a thrilling saloon car race with Frank Gardner's 5-litre Boss Mustang winning from David Piper's Camaro and Chris Craft's Escort. John Fitzpatrick in a Mini-Cooper took the smaller saloon race from Gordon Spice, and Roger Nathan took sports car honours in his Astra.

The court injunction imposed on the circuit in 1953 had expired by 1970 and the GLC took it upon themselves to promote more meetings, increasing the permitted days for racing from five to 14. The Thames Estuary Auto Club were first to take advantage of this, running a clubman's meeting including a variety of saloon and single-seater races on June 13. A quieter event took place on July 11, when the Aston Martin Owners' Club celebrated the 50th anniversary of the marque with a Jubilee Festival. A day of nostalgia for Aston enthusiasts included a parade and concours d'elegance with cars from the 1923 two-seaters to the latest Volante taking part. Several sports-racers from the 1950s were there, as well as Neil Corner's DBR4 Grand Prix car.

Club motorcycle racers benefited from the extra racing days too, with a bike meeting squeezed in on August 1 for the Racing 50 MCC. Bike fans were back again at the end of the month, on August 31, for the Bank Holiday 'Bemsee' meeting. The lap records took a real hammering that afternoon as Paul Smart, Pat Mahoney, Martin Ashwood and Ray Pickrell all made their mark in the book. For the first time a Team Challenge race was tried at the Palace, with riders racing in pairs. Paul Smart (Triumph Trident) took the win and lap record with his team-mate Ron Chandler (Seeley) third to give them overall victory. Next best pairing were Dave Nixon and Peter Butler on Boyer Triumphs. By the end of the afternoon, new records had been established in all classes racing except the sidecars, so the crowd left well satisfied with the event.

Forward Trust Finance backed the meeting held on September 13, ably organized by the BARC, televised by the BBC and soaked by the elements. Heat 1 of the Formula 3 race was held on a damp track and was a runaway win for Dave Walker's Gold Leaf Lotus from the March of Dave Morgan. Heat 2 was run in appalling conditions, with

Carlos Pace initially leading the pack. Andy Sutcliffe splashed by on lap 3 but lost it at North Tower, thumping the sleepers hard and bending his Lotus. He was immediately joined by the Brabhams of Gerry Birrell and David Purley, and then Fritz Jordan spun off at The Link. Just four drivers were left on the streaming track, hardly daring to change up out of first gear, the leader, Pace, driving with one hand over the engine air intake to keep the water out. By lap 5, Tony Birchenough had pulled out and Pace, Bev Bond (GLTL Lotus) and Chris Skeaping (Chevron) were relieved when the race was stopped. The track had dried out a bit for the final but most drivers still preferred to use wet-weather tyres. Pace made the best start pursued by Dave Walker (on dry tyres), Wilson Fittipaldi (Lotus), Dave Morgan, Bev Bond and Cyd Williams (Brabham). Walker chased the Brazilian driver but hit a wet patch on lap 16 at New Link and bent the car. Meanwhile Cyd Williams had been making up ground and with five laps left he was second and closing on Pace, finishing 3 seconds behind him at the flag.

The Vespa Club held a scooter rally on September 27, and circuit manager Allan Tyler was horrified to discover that many of the scooterists had turned up with highly modified machines and proposed to race them. Not all the

Frank Gardner's Boss 302 Mustang leads Dennis Leach's similar car and a pair of Camaros into North Tower Crescent during the Group 2 saloon race at the Alcoa Trophy meeting in May 1970 ... and a few seconds later Leach gets it all wrong at North Tower, causing considerable consternation amongst the group of pursuing Escort drivers as Gardner breaks clear of the pack and heads for another victory.

scooters were the quiet runabouts he had envisaged when he gave the go-ahead for the meeting!

The 1970 car season concluded with the *Daily Express* meeting on October 3. This meeting will always be remembered for the incident at the last corner of the last lap of the Formula 3 final. The race was led from flag to flag by Dave Walker's Lotus, but snapping at his heels was a battling pack comprised of James Hunt (Lotus 59), Mike Beuttler, Tony Trimmer and Gerry Birrell in Brabhams, and the white March 703 of Dave Morgan. As they approached South Tower for the final time, Hunt and Morgan both left their braking to the last possible moment (or perhaps a bit later). The two cars collided in the corner and the March ripped both righthand wheels off the Lotus. Morgan parked his crippled car against the pit wall sleepers, marshals tried to stop the errant wheels, and the other competitors swerved around the wreckage. Hunt climbed from his car, stationary in the middle of the track, ran after Morgan and knocked him flat with a punch. Meanwhile, Beuttler, Trimmer and Birrell had followed Walker across the line to fill the places.

The whole incident came before the RAC who decided that Morgan was guilty of reckless driving and imposed a fine and ban on him. Many felt that Morgan was harshly treated and that, although he may have been over enthusiastic in his attempts to beat Hunt to the line, the competitiveness of both drivers and the closely matched performance of the Formula 3 cars of the day made an accident of this sort almost inevitable. Although incidents like this also helped to get James Hunt his nickname 'Hunt the Shunt', his total bill for crash repairs in the 1970 season was only £600, and the Crystal Palace affair cost him £400 of that.

The 1970 season closed with another extra event taking advantage of the expiry of the court injunction. Karting enthusiasts had for some time been keen to hold races at the Palace, but when there were only five meetings a year it was impossible. Allan Tyler shared their enthusiasm and the members of the British Kart Club now threw themselves into the organization of a race meeting. The cost of staging a meeting at the Palace would have been too great for the relatively small club but they managed to secure backing from the makers of Players No 6 cigarettes and the event was incorporated into the London Karting Weekend. There was an RAC Karting Conference on the afternoon of Friday, October 16, followed by a grand party, the 'World of Karting Gala', in the Seymour Hall in the evening. Hopefully not too many drivers had hangovers as they assembled at Crystal Palace next morning for the racing.

Emerson Fittipaldi drove a Formula 2 Lotus for the private Bardahl team in 1970 and found himself busy signing autographs in the Crystal Palace paddock, a task he would have to perform more frequently two years later when he won the first of his two World Championships.

Towards the end of its active life the Crystal Palace race circuit occasionally echoed to a different sound as hordes of karters took to the track for some highly competitive racing, amongst them several drivers who would later graduate to successful careers as racing drivers. Those walls on the outside of corners must have looked quite forbidding from such a low driving position.

Some of them went on to drive at Tilbury on the Sunday morning. It was a veritable karting feast and the BKC advertised the event widely. They knew that despite sponsorship the meeting would run at a loss but the prestige of racing on a long circuit, and one as famous as the Palace, outweighed the financial risk. There were some worries about safety but the sleeper barriers were faced with straw bales as at motorcycle meetings, and some 260 drivers entered, including all the top names, among them Les Sheppard, Reg Gange, Dave Ferris and Martin Hines. Nigel Mansell was there, then just 16 and racing a Dale-Villiers 200, and so were Tony and Tim Brise, following in the footsteps of father Johnny Brise. Tim won the 250 International event, lapping at over 80mph. The kart racers made a big impression on the spectators who got tremendous value for money, with a race every 12 minutes or so and superb organization by the BKC.

Easter Monday fell on April 12 in 1971, and the ACU were in charge for their usual season opener. Then came the now customary Spring Bank Holiday International Formula 2 meeting, this year sponsored by Hilton Transport. The high quality entry list included Graham Hill, James Hunt, Derek Bell and John Watson amongst others, but the winner of the final was the brilliant young Brazilian Emerson Fittipaldi. Tim Schenken was second and Ronnie Peterson third. The lap record set the previous year, jointly held by Jochen Rindt and Jackie Stewart at 49.6 seconds, 100.89mph, was equalled by no less than four drivers, Schenken, Peterson, Fittipaldi and Jaussaud.

During this period, circuit owners from all over the UK were all looking for something different in motor racing to help bring back the crowds which had dwindled away, and they met regularly at the Steering Wheel Club in Mayfair to discuss events and possibilities. Allan Tyler, as the Crystal Palace circuit manager, attended these meetings and one idea to emerge was evening racing. Many sporting events took place in the evening – football, athletics, speedway, boxing – and always attracted big crowds. Crystal Palace seemed the ideal venue for an evening race meeting, close to where people worked and lived in large numbers, and of course back in the 1920s some very successful evening path race meetings had been held. Originally a Wednesday evening was chosen for the first such event, but finally the date was set for Friday, June 18, 1971. It was billed as the 'Trumps Moto-Pop' meeting and as well as motor racing there were to be side shows, exhibitions, a fun fair, a barbecue and a beer garden. After the racing, there would be a pop concert from Manfred Mann, and Desmond Dekker and the Aces, and jazz from Humphrey Lyttelton. Trumps, who sponsored the event, ran employment agencies and holiday centres, and the company saw it as an afternoon and evening filled with attractions for everyone. They arranged fashion shows on lorries to tour the circuit between races, promoting clothes from their parent company, Peter Robinson. There was even to be a marbles match, world champions against a team of *Penthouse* Pets and model girls. The other circuit owners no doubt looked on with interest to see how successful the experiment would be.

What should have been a 'Midsummer Night's Motor Racing' turned into a complete washout: the weather was appalling and the attendance consequently very poor. There was an afternoon practice session for the racers and the track was so wet that the Formula 3 drivers, who included David Purley, James Hunt, Alan Jones and Roger Williamson, could lap barely faster than the karts. Many drivers decided to go home there and then, rather than risk damage to their cars in non-championship racing, especially as there was a Lombank Championship Formula 3 race the following Sunday at Brands Hatch. The depleted Formula 3 grid had a shortened race for the Chris Moore Memorial Trophy and through the gloom James Hunt's brand new March 713 was an easy winner, with Roger Williamson's similar car in second place after a race-long dice with the Puma-BRM of Bob Evans. As well as Formula 3 and karts, there were modified sports cars, saloons, and a special ladies' race, and cars spun off in all five events. The fashion parades were abandoned, the barbecue and fun fair washed away, and the whole exercise was a complete financial disaster for the sponsor, Trumps, whose managing director lost his job. The evening race meeting was never repeated at the Palace, or at any other circuit, which was rather a shame as the idea and the promotional effort behind it deserved better. Perhaps it was just expecting too much of the fickle English summer weather. . .

Formula 3 still provided the mainstay of racing at the Palace, and was top of the bill for the *Daily Express* Petonyer Trophy meeting on August 7, organized by the BRSCC.

The *Daily Express* gave lots of publicity to the meetings it backed at the Palace, sometimes to the surprise of other circuit operators, in particular Silverstone, who hosted the *Daily Express* International Trophy every spring. A small but very enthusiastic band in the Crystal Palace office fed the paper with as much information as they possibly could, and the *Express* was only too happy to use it.

The racing on this occasion was full of incident, the showery weather leaving the Formula 3 teams uncertain about what tyres to use. James Hunt (March) kept clear of the crashes behind him to win Heat 1 despite having his car jammed in third gear for much of the race. Heat 2 was notable for a start-line shunt: pole man Dave Walker (Lotus) and Brendan McInerney (March) beside him were slow away, the latter missing a gear, but behind them Jose Ferreira got a flyer in his Brabham-Novamotor and hit Walker's Lotus very hard, the two cars then collecting the Lotus-Holbay of Rikki von Opel. All three cars were out of the race within yards of the start and the field was further reduced when Chris O'Brien crashed into the sleepers at North Tower on lap 8 and needed hospital treatment. Through the debris Alan McCully (Lotus-Vegantune) picked his way to victory. There was another shower of rain before the final and more uncertainty about tyres. Hunt led at the start from Williamson, McCully and Steve Thompson's Ensign. On lap 2 McCully had a moment at North Tower, frightening Thompson who hit the barrier taking avoiding action. At New Link, Hunt went sideways and was hit by Andy Sutcliffe who then collected McCully. All this left Roger Williamson to take a comfortable win and the £300 prize money, with Chris Skeaping (Chevron) second and Alan Jones (Brabham) third.

The two-wheelers were back on Bank Holiday Monday, September 4, riders at the 'Bemsee' meeting including Paul Smart, Barry Ditchburn and Peter Williams who took a win on his Norton Commando. Then a week later, on September 11, the Formula 3 circus returned once again for the Iberia Airlines Trophy meeting. Heat 1 saw some

John Fitzpatrick recalls his tyre-smoking Mini-racing days with some spectacular cornering in his Escort at North Tower during the Hilton Trophy meeting in 1971 as Rod Mansfield peers through the smokescreen at the wheel of another Escort.

Ronnie Peterson leads the field into North Tower Crescent at the start of Heat 2 of the Formula 2 race at the 1971 Spring Bank Holiday meeting at the wheel of his March-Ford.

Just over two months later James Hunt held a narrow lead over ultimate winner Roger Williamson, both of them in Formula 3 March-Ford 713s, as they streamed through South Tower Corner at the August meeting.

A study in formation flying. Barry Ditchburn on his 354cc Broad Yamaha holding a tenuous lead over the 496cc Kirby Metisse of Jim Harvey as they sweep through South Tower Corner and on to the start-finish straight in their 500cc race in September 1971.

Rex Butcher and his Ivy Yamaha emerging from The Glade fractionally ahead of eventual winner Stanley Woods, also Yamaha-mounted, in their 250cc race at the same meeting.

A mixed field for the 350cc event. In race order are Rex Butcher and his 348cc Ivy Yamaha (7), Paul Smart on a 348cc JF Yamaha (1), John Riley and his 250cc Broad Yamaha (143), Brian Wackett, 350cc Chuck Seeley (103), Clive Offer, 346cc Yamaha (17), Tony Hierons, 350cc Kawasaki (112) and Robin Gray, 344cc Aermacchi (116).

Martin Carney takes the tight line at North Tower Crescent on his 350cc Yamsel to try to find a way past Brian Wackett's 350cc Seeley, both riders making good use of the shoulders of their tyres.

The beginning of a long walk home. Dave Walker and his tyre-smoking Lotus 69 arrive at North Tower sandwiched between the Merlyn of Jody Scheckter (left) and the Brabham BT35 of Colin Vandervell during their Formula 3 race in September 1971...

...and a minute or two later Walker, Scheckter and Vandervell head back towards the paddock having left their tangled cars at the trackside.

furious dicing between the Gold Leaf Team Lotus car of Dave Walker, Roger Williamson's March and the Brabham of Colin Vandervell. Walker and Vandervell in particular traded the lead several times before a tail-ender slowed the Brabham driver, allowing the Lotus to take the flag. In Heat 2 another battle was fought, between James Hunt (March), on pole, Andy Sutcliffe (Lotus), Jody Scheckter (Merlyn) and Barrie Maskell (Chevron). Sutcliffe, Hunt and Scheckter all had a turn in front until the Lotus retired with a slipping clutch, leaving Hunt and Scheckter, two future World Champions, to dice for the rest of the race, Hunt winning by just two-tenths of a second. Hunt stalled on the grid in the final and it was Vandervell who led through North Tower from Walker, Williamson, Purley (Ensign) and Scheckter. The race resolved into a duel between Vandervell and Walker, and Scheckter broke the lap record catching them. By lap 15 the three cars were nose-to-tail, Brabham leading from Lotus and Merlyn. On the penultimate lap they arrived at North Tower together in a cloud of tyre smoke, wheels interlocked. Vandervell and Walker hit the sleeper barrier, Scheckter initially carried on but had to stop at New Link with a wheel awry. Suddenly Roger Williamson and David Purley found themselves racing for the lead. Purley was in front at the start of the last lap but it was Williamson who took the win.

Two weeks later local residents had another noisy Saturday when the Aston Martin Owners' Club promoted a historic car race meeting. While there had been historic races at the Palace before, this was the first all-historic event. Another first was a roller speed skating competition before the car racing began, the male participants completing three full laps of the circuit (over four miles) on skates! The ladies had to make do with a short race along the top straight. But the cars were what most people had come to see and there was an entry overflowing with classic racers including a Birdcage Maserati for Hon Patrick Lindsay, an Aston Martin DBR1/2 for Neil Corner, and examples of ERA, Jaguar D-Type, Lister-Jaguar, Ferrari GTO, Talbot Lago, Maserati 250F and Lotus 16. The Palace was reliving its history – but the show was coming to an end.

The season closed with a kart meeting on October 16, the British Kart Club having decided to go ahead with a second race day despite the financial loss sustained at the first and the fact that Players had withdrawn their support. Stringent economies were made, but the club managed to attract over 270 entries so a good day's racing was in prospect. The weather was showery and the track slippery with fallen leaves, and the behaviour of some drivers, overtaking under yellow flags and generally ignoring signals, left much to be desired. The big fields and the sheer speed of the karts made quite a spectacle and the racing was fast and furious, but there were many incidents and the ambulance crews had a busy day. Fortunately, though, the worst injuries were broken ankles.

A few weeks before the beginning of the 1972 season

came the inevitable announcement from the GLC Arts and Recreation Committee: after the season was over Crystal Palace would host motor racing no more. Many reasons were put forward for the closure, and some of them had been evident to the perceptive observer for a long time, but it was nevertheless a very sad turn of events for the Palace enthusiasts, particularly in view of the recent increased activity at the circuit.

However, one more busy season had been planned, and it kicked off in the usual style on Easter Monday, April 3. The *Daily Express* backed this ACU-organized bike meeting and helped to promote it with a display of racing machinery in its Fleet Street office. The entry contained all the familiar names including Charlie Sandby, Martin Ashwood, Pat Mahoney, Barry Ditchburn, Dave Potter and Dave Nixon.

The final international race meeting at the Palace was held on Spring Bank Holiday Monday, May 29, 1972, and it was the fifth round of the European Formula 2 Championship. The atmosphere was rather gloomy with closure looming but the quality of the entry ensured that the Palace would go out on a high note. The chairman of the GLC Arts and Recreation Committee, H Sebag-Montefiore, wrote of the impending closure in the programme, and circuit manager Allan Tyler contributed a

review of past seasons. A clash of dates with the Oulton Park Gold Cup kept away a few regular competitors including Fittipaldi, Schenken, Peterson and Wisell, but the rest of the Formula 2 brigade were there including five 'graded' drivers, men who had scored points on two or more occasions in the previous Formula 1 season. Local hero John Surtees was making a welcome return to the circuit, not having raced there since 1967, now the constructor as well as the driver of his own cars, and the others were Graham Hill, Francois Cevert, Henri Pescarolo and Jean-Pierre Beltoise who had won a very wet Monaco Grand Prix in a BRM a fortnight earlier. Three other drivers, Vic Elford, with the works Chevron, Andrea de Adamich in a Fina-sponsored Surtees, and Jochen Mass, driving the STP March in place of Ronnie Peterson, had a specially busy weekend as they were competing in a sports car race at the Nürburgring on the Sunday and flew back and forth between the two circuits for qualifying and racing.

Other non-graded drivers, the only ones eligible for points in the championship, included Mike Hailwood joining fellow former motorcycle racer John Surtees in his team with sponsorship from the Lesney Matchbox toy company. Mike was racing at the Palace on four wheels for the first time, not having visited the circuit since 1957. Jody

The close-fought battles between Jody Scheckter in his Impact McLaren and Mike Hailwood in his Surtees in both their heat and the final of the Formula 2 race were highlights of the last International race meeting held at Crystal Palace in May 1972. Here Scheckter is narrowly ahead as Hailwood takes an armful of opposite-lock through South Tower Corner.

At North Tower the positions have been reversed, but although Hailwood went on to win his heat, the final went to Scheckter after both drivers had put on a great display of sustained on-the-limit driving.

Scheckter was in the works Impact McLaren, a young Austrian called Niki Lauda, who had borrowed a large amount of money from the bank in order to race, was driving the second STP March, Carlos Reutemann was in the Rondel Racing entry, Emerson Fittipaldi's brother Wilson had a Brabham and his fellow Brazilian Carlos Pace a Pygmee. Dave Morgan, the surprise winner of the first round of the championship at Mallory Park, his first Formula 2 race, was entered in a private Brabham. John Watson was down to drive the unique Tui, entered by New Zealander Alan McCall, the first time the car had appeared since its former regular driver Bert Hawthorne had been killed at Hockenheim.

It was perhaps no surprise that John Surtees should break another lap record at the Palace taking pole position for Heat 1 with J-P Beltoise and Patrick Depailler alongside him. As the flag fell, Niki Lauda leapt away from row 3 to get behind Surtees and Beltoise. Graham Hill's Brabham was hit by another car and turned sideways on the grid, and the March of Gerry Birrell, unable to avoid him, was launched over the top. Hill's helmet received a tyre mark to add to the familiar London Rowing Club colours and Birrell's car ran along the top of the sleeper barrier before crashing onto the track and shedding two wheels. Hill was whisked off to hospital for an X-ray on his shoulder. The two written-off cars created an additional hazard as the competitors completed the first lap with Beltoise just ahead of Surtees, Lauda, Depailler and Mike Beuttler. The wreckage was cleared out of the way as a tremendous battle raged at the front of the field: this was the last international at the Palace and everyone wanted to win it! The Brabham of Beltoise was under increasing pressure from John Surtees, whilst just behind Lauda, Depailler and Beuttler were racing hard. A little further back, Wilson Fittipaldi had clawed his way up from a lowly grid position to join the group disputing seventh place consisting of Richard Scott (Brabham), Tom Walkinshaw (GRD), John Watson (Tui) and Vic Elford (Chevron). After five laps the Surtees driven by Carlos Reusch pulled off at North Tower and two laps later Big John's car suffered a similar fate. Beltoise now had a more comfortable lead and when Niki Lauda also pulled out he seemed to be heading for a certain win, with fellow Frenchman Depailler behind. Mike Beuttler in third place was dropping back, losing power with a broken exhaust, and Carlos Reutemann in the Rondel Racing Brabham was closing in. Behind them, Walkinshaw had joined the retirements but Richard Scott was hanging on just ahead of a fierce struggle between Elford, Fittipaldi and Watson. Then

Richard Scott (Brabham), Vic Elford (Chevron), David Purley (Brabham), John Watson (Tui) and Bob Wollek (Brabham) nose-to-tail though North Tower Crescent during the last and one of the best of Crystal Palace's Formula 2 races.

Graham Hill applies some opposite-lock during practice for the May 1972 Formula 2 race with his Brabham, but he was destined to become the first race retirement when his car was hit by another as they left the grid, turned sideways, and was then run over by a third car, Hill ending up in hospital for a precautionary X-ray.

Yet another victory in the making as Hillman Imp expert Ray Calcutt leads a bunch of Minis through The Glade during a close-fought Special Saloon race at the first of two meetings held in September 1972.

Reutemann took Beuttler for third, rapidly caught Depailler, and the two of them closed on Beltoise. On lap 24 the Argentinian took the two French drivers, Beltoise heading for the pits with a puncture and resuming in seventh place. Reutemann now began to pull away and was handed a comfortable win when Depailler's March blew its engine in front of the pits. Beuttler's ailing car was passed by Elford, and it looked as if Watson would be third but he slowed as the water temperature went off the clock, allowing Scott through. Adrian Wilkins was fifth as Beuttler stopped on his final lap, being classified seventh, and Beltoise was rewarded with sixth place. What a race – and it was only the first heat!

Heat 2 had Francois Cevert in the John Coombs Elf March on pole, with the Impact McLaren of Jody Scheckter, who was suffering from flu, and the Fina Surtees of Andrea de Adamich completing the front row. Cevert rocketed away as the flag fell with Scheckter and de Adamich behind. Then came Mike Hailwood in the Matchbox Surtees, followed by Jochen Mass (March), Jean-Pierre Jaussaud (Brabham) and the rest. By lap 6 Cevert was leaving a plume of oil smoke in his wake and stopped just past the pits thinking an oil pipe had broken. John Coombs quickly investigated and found the cam cover loose and Cevert returned the car to the pits for attention, rejoining way down the field. Pescarolo was another Frenchman in trouble, with a bad misfire. Mike the Bike was now pursuing the leading McLaren and the pair treated the crowd to some super racing as they scrapped for the lead. Jaussaud displaced Mass from fourth place, Bob Wollek (Brabham) was sixth and David Purley (LEC March) had recovered from an awful start to reach seventh, although a spin at North Tower dropped him back down the field. On lap 28 Dick Barker crashed his Brabham into the sleepers at North Tower and the car caught fire as the tank split. The marshals were quick to extinguish the flames as the driver leapt out, having burnt his hand slightly. Up front, Scheckter was forced to slow when his visor was covered in oil as he lapped Tom Belso's Brabham which was smoking badly on its way to retirement. This allowed Hailwood into the lead and he pulled out a 4-second gap on his way to the flag. Scheckter was happy enough with second place, and behind them came de Adamich, Wollek, Purley and Silvio Moser.

Next, the smaller capacity saloons came out for their race, Jonathan Buncombe's Mini-Cooper winning from the similar car of Rob Mason, while in the paddock the 16 Formula 2 finalists prepared to do battle. The first six finishers from each heat plus the next four fastest were the qualifiers. First reserve Francois Cevert scraped in at the

Crystal Palace tended to be a great leveller of horsepower. Here Martin Birrane has to work hard at the wheel of his Ford Mustang to stave off the challenge of David Matthews and his Broadspeed Escort.

Frank Gardner in a typically exuberant drive behind the left-handed steering wheel of his Camaro during Crystal Palace's final season of racing.

Dave Potter (10) and Graham Sharp (9) on their 754cc Kuhn Nortons pursued by David Nixon and his 741cc Boyer Trident during the final motorcycle race meeting at Crystal Palace in August 1972.

Right, up the hill for the last time. Anthony Garrioch and his AJS (103) and John Watson and his Yamaha (93) lead a bunch of riders up Maxim Rise during the final 350cc race.

back as poor Andrea de Adamich crashed his Surtees on the warm-up lap. Scheckter led away with Hailwood, Reutemann, Elford, Scott, Purley and Watson in pursuit through North Tower. Mike Beuttler was spun sideways in the melee and then struck hard by the Brabham of Beltoise, the Frenchman continuing at the back but poor Beuttler stepping out of a two-wheeled March. The crowd were on their feet as Scheckter built a small lead, opposite-locking through South Tower, but soon Hailwood began to close on the McLaren. Behind came Reutemann and then Vic Elford fighting hard to stay ahead of Scott and Purley. Watson was in trouble as the water temperature rose again, signifying a blown head gasket. By lap 13 Hailwood was hounding Scheckter and cheers went up as he found a way past. Both men were keen to win this race, neither having won in F2 before, and when Scheckter spun approaching North Tower it looked good for the Surtees driver. But a broken anti-roll bar was causing Mike severe handling problems. Scheckter quickly recovered and set about chasing the new leader, whilst Elford closed upon Reutemann. Further back, Purley had broken a drive shaft and tried to push his car from Ramp Bend to the pits. Seven laps from home, the Surtees and McLaren were nose-to-tail, Scheckter trying everything to pass. On lap 47 the cars were side by side past the pits with Scheckter on the outside round the kink before North Tower and he was able to outbrake Hailwood into the turn and accelerate into the Glade ahead. Mike could do no more and had to be content with second place, though he had some consolation in having set fastest lap during his heat, 48.4 seconds, 103.39mph, the outright record which would now stand for all time. Reutemann just held off Elford for third, with Cevert and Beltoise fifth and sixth. The crowd were enthralled and the Palace reputation for close and exciting racing was being maintained to the last.

There was still the large capacity saloon race to come, the Wiggins Teape Paperchase, and the imminent arrival of the rain which had been threatening all day meant some last-minute decisions about tyres on the grid. Brian Muir pleased the sponsors of both the race and his car when the 'Papermakers Pacemaker' Ford Capri narrowly beat the similar car of Gerry Birrell, who was making up for his disastrous Formula 2 race. The rain gave the drivers a real problem, as most had started on slick tyres, but at least the resulting dramatic action meant that those spectators who had braved the weather were well rewarded.

The summer continued with the Palace hosting the RAC 'L' Driver of the Year competition and a Veteran Car Club rally, and on August 12 the BRSCC ran the Petonyer Trophy meeting, with the usual close-fought Formula 3 race topping the bill. On Bank Holiday Monday, August 28, the last-ever motorcycle meeting was held, with 'Bemsee' in charge. The programme contained a booklet compiled by circuit manager Allan Tyler describing motorcycle racing at the Palace since 1927, and the sadness of the occasion was lightened both by a superb entry and by the arrival of a host of riders of yesteryear with vintage machines to give a nostalgic atmosphere to the proceedings. It was a day to remember as Eric Oliver, Jock West, George Rowley, Arthur Wheeler and Denis Glover amongst others paraded their vintage bikes. Then the modern racers entertained the crowd with 15 races, Dave Potter taking the production win on his Gus Kuhn Commando and George O'Dell a couple of sidecar wins. Dave Potter, Dave Nixon and Graham Sharp provided the thrills in every race they met up in, especially the Team Challenge Race where Nixon's three-cylinder Boyer Triumph scored a narrow win over Sharp's Kuhn Norton and team-mate Dave Potter cruised home third with a rod through the crankcase of his Kuhn Norton. John Wilkinson's 1937 Norton won the vintage event, evoking memories of great Palace races in the past. The day finished with the All-Comers Grand Finale, and once again Potter, Sharp and Nixon scrapped for the honours, all determined to win the last-ever motorcycle race at the Palace. After 15 laps it was Dave Nixon on his Boyer Triumph who wrote his name in the record book, just four-tenths of a second ahead of Graham Sharp's Kuhn Norton. His lap of honour

Current British Saloon Car Champion Bill McGovern cocks a fat front wheel and tyre of his Bevan-prepared Sunbeam Imp during a race in May 1972. In those days GLC officials at Crystal Palace were less than ideally kitted-out for work at a race track!

ceremonially closed the circuit for motorcycle racing and the crowd dispersed in melancholy mood.

For the car racing fans there were just a couple more meetings. On September 9 the BARC arrived with the Hexagon Trophy meeting. Sponsors Hexagon, based in Highgate, North London, were dealers in high performance cars, keen on motor sport to enhance their image, and within two years they would be running their own Formula 1 Brabham for John Watson. At this Palace meeting Formula 3 was the principal attraction, though cold showery weather and the impending closure meant the crowd was small and the atmosphere gloomy. Mike Walker won the first F3 heat in an Ensign, designed by former racer Mo Nunn, and Russell Wood the second in a March. The final proved fairly hectic. On the first lap Mike Wilds' Dempster Developments Ensign was pushed hard into the sleeper wall at North Tower and a little later Heat 2 winner Wood crashed out at Park Curve. This left Mike Walker in the lead, a position made more secure when Tony Brise (GRD), Roger Williamson (GRD) and Bob Evans (March), who had been part of a large group, had a coming together at South Tower. Behind the leading Ensign came Jochen Mass (March), Peter Hull (Brabham) and Tony Trimmer (JPS Lotus). When Mass spun at Park Curve he dropped to

fourth and the finishing order was established. So Mike Walker was the last Formula 3 winner at the Palace, his works Ensign some way ahead of Peter Hull. Supporting races were for Super Vee single-seaters, won easily by Brian Henton in a Crossle, for sports GT cars, won by Martin Raymond's Chevron, and three saloon events which provided wins for Ray Calcutt (Imp), Chris Bruce (Cooper S) and Gerry Marshall (Vauxhall Firenza), the latter entertaining the crowd with a spirited duel with Mike Crabtree's Escort.

And so the day arrived. Saturday, September 23, 1972, the end of an era. The Aston Martin Owners' Club organized their *Daily Mirror* Historic Car Race Meeting, calling it a 'Farewell to Crystal Palace Circuit'. The Hon Gerald Lascelles wrote an appreciation in the programme, recalling that the Palace...

'has filled a unique role in British racing history. It is the only circuit owned by a municipality, and the only one sited within the confines of a major city. With hindsight one could argue, with a touch of irony, that these two factors contributed most to the decision to close the circuit. Modern racing machinery, for all its advanced sophistication, does not generate the quietest scene on earth: nor does its greatly enhanced speed factor ease the

118

problem of the circuit owner in containing the cars from the public viewing areas. With these two factors weighing heavily against its retention, it was perhaps inevitable that a council not over orientated in motor sport enthusiasm should take the decision to close the track.'

The meeting was heavily over-subscribed and about 150 would-be entrants had to be turned away. As at the final motorcycle meeting a month previously, many famous names from the past were there to say a fond farewell to the circuit. Late summer sunshine bathed the park and, fittingly, the leaves on the trees had begun to turn to autumn gold. A large crowd watched as the meeting began with a parade of notable cars and drivers. Raymond Mays was reunited with his ERA, the first of many to lap the old 2-mile circuit in under 2 minutes. Wilkie Wilkinson was there with a Cooper-Bristol, Alec Issigonis, best remembered as the designer of the Mini, drove his Lightweight Special, Paul Emery had one of his Emerysons and there was another ERA for Ian Connell. Others taking part included Innes Ireland, winner of the last Formula 1 race on the track, Stirling Moss, Mike Salmon, Graham Whitehead, George Abecassis, and drivers from more recent seasons like Harry Stiller, Mark Konig and Ed Nelson. Roy Salvadori was there to remember numerous wins in the past, and there were many others.

The races which followed had a fine entry of historic and classic cars, the first being won by David Llewelyn's huge 8.3-litre Bentley. The final rounds of several championships were included, with close points tables ensuring keen racing. In the first sports car race, Chris Drake (Lotus-Bristol Mk10) and the similar car of Peter van Rossem

engaged in a furious dice with the Mk1 Lola-Climax of David Beckett. Van Rossem had already survived a spin at Ramp Bend as the trio entered the final lap still swapping places. At Ramp, Beckett took the outside line, led Drake up the hill towards South Tower and, right on and momentarily over the limit, with some hairy sideways motoring, he managed to cross the line first. Van Rossem had another spin at South Tower but still finished third.

For the Seven Seas Fellowship Challenge Trophy race there were nine ERAs on the grid, reviving memories of the first car races at Crystal Palace back in April 1937, when Pat Fairfield had won the Coronation Trophy. His very car, ERA R4A, was on the front row, driven now by John Venables-Llewelyn. Martin Morris with his 'B' type ERA led from flag to flag, with Venables-Llewelyn behind him. Another ERA, Hamish Moffat's, came home third, having been hard pressed initially by Ray Potter in the Delage-ERA which Roy Salvadori had raced in the first postwar Palace meeting. As Potter's challenge faded in the closing stages he was passed by Pat Lindsay in the ex-Bira ERA Remus and by Peter Waller in yet another ERA. Amongst the cars further back was the amazing 24-litre Bentley-Napier of Peter Morley and Robert Cooper's P3 Alfa Romeo, once driven by Nuvolari and Varzi.

A race for 'modern' monoposto cars had been marred in practice when Michael Irons had struck the sleepers very hard with his Brabham BT18 and had been taken to hospital with a broken leg – at least he could claim to be the last victim of the unyielding barriers! Trevor Scarrett led throughout from pole with his similar Brabham. Then came

One of the largest cars ever to race at Crystal Palace was also one of the last to appear there. This is Peter Morley at the wheel of his 24-litre Bentley-Napier being pursued on its final run on September 23, 1972.

a second race for 'Vintage and Venerable' cars which Andy McLennan won in his MG N-Type.

A 15-lap race for historic single-seaters competing for the *Daily Mirror* Trophy brought a wonderful collection of cars to the grid, mostly postwar machines but with several ERAs and Cooper's beautiful P3 Alfa getting a second outing. Neil Corner was in pole position with his Aston Martin DBR4 and beside him with the scarlet Maserati 250F was Charles Lucas, making a welcome return to racing. The spectators were reminded of the mid-1950s when both Peter Collins and Stirling Moss had won the London Trophy in similar Maseratis and Roy Salvadori had driven one to many victories. Further back came an assortment of other Maseratis, a couple of Connaughts, a Lotus 16, a Ferrari 625 and some Cooper-Bristols. At the flag 'Luke' made a terrific start and the red Maserati led the green Aston Martin into North Tower, but Corner came out in front. Lucas never gave up trying to pass Neil Corner's car and treated the

crowd to some heart-stopping opposite lock slides just inches from the sleeper barriers. Despite his tremendous efforts he was unable to retake the British car and finished some 2½ seconds behind, with Bill Wilks in the Lotus 16 third and Allan Cottam's 1953 Connaught fourth. The penultimate race was the final round of the Cussons Classic GT series and was dominated by Willie Green in a gorgeous 1962 Ferrari 250 GTO, the sound of its V12 engine echoing off the whitewashed sleepers. Behind came James Mehew in the unique Bizzarini Le Mans and Chris Spencer-Phillips in an AC Daytona.

Just after 6pm the cars were assembling on the grid, for the last time at Crystal Palace, for the AMOC Historic Sports Car race. Willie Green was already confirmed as JCB Champion, so it was a straightforward race for the honour of the last win. On pole position was burly Gerry Marshall in the Hexagon of Highgate Lister-Jaguar, the last one ever built (recent replicas aside), and beside him were two

The field gets away for the 15-lap *Daily Mirror* Trophy race for historic racing cars at the final Crystal Palace meeting, with Charles Lucas and his Maserati 250F neck-and-neck with the Aston Martin DBR4 which Neil Corner had put on pole position.

A contrast in cornering styles. Charles Lucas powers his Maserati 250F through South Tower Corner on opposite-lock as he comes up to challenge Willie Eckerslyke, whose Ferrari 625 is taking a wider line with just a touch of understeer.

Through the twists of Maxim Rise, Simpson's Cooper-Bristol leads Rose's Maserati 250F, Eckerslyke's Ferrari 625 and the remainder of the field during the *Daily Mirror* Trophy race.

Birdcage Maseratis, Nick Faure with another Hexagon entry and Willie Green in Anthony Bamford's car. Behind them were a host of other historic cars, including Richard Bond's ex-Jim Clark Lister-Jaguar, two Ferrari 410s for Colin Crabbe and Chris Renwick, and a Maserati tipo 60 for Alain de Cadenet, as well as examples of Jaguar XK120, XK150 and D-Type, and others. Tom Fletcher had a Lister making its first appearance since the owner had begun its restoration about eight years earlier.

Richard Bond got a flying start from row 2 and the cars arrived at North Tower three abreast. At the end of the first lap Bond had dropped back as Nick Faure (Maserati), Gerry Marshall (Lister-Jaguar) and Willie Green (Maserati) broke away. They circulated nose-to-tail, with armfuls of opposite lock, until half-distance when Marshall squeezed past Faure. Headlights blazing, the big man gave a show of superb driving. With two laps to go Nick Faure was displaced into third spot by Willie Green who tried very hard to catch the Lister but to no avail. As he exited South Tower for the last time Gerry Marshall raised his hand in triumph to go down in the record book as the winner of the last race at Crystal Palace. Willie Green was 1.4 seconds behind, with Faure a close third, Bond fourth, John Harper fifth in the ex-Archie Scott-Brown Lister-Jaguar prototype, and Anthony Hutton sixth.

As Gerry Marshall set off on his lap of honour, the gathering twilight brought a unique chapter of motor racing history to a close. The crowd left well satisfied with an excellent day of racing superbly organized by the AMOC, but saddened at the thought that they could not return in the spring of 1973 to the special atmosphere that only Crystal Palace could offer. The official press release had said that Brands Hatch and Thruxton provided the London racegoer with an alternative, but somehow they could never replace the Palace, just a few miles from the heart of London.

On October 21 the British Kart Club held their third and final meeting at the circuit, and after that the sound of racing was heard there no more. The venue continued to be used occasionally for other car club gatherings, as it had been during the racing years. There was a regular Alvis Day, for example, between 1958 and 1974, with hotly contested autotests round pylons set out on part of the track. One Alvis owner recalls that it never rained for that event – would that the racers had been so lucky! In 1977 competition cars visited the Palace briefly when it formed a stage on the Southern Car Club's Happy Eater Southern Rally, run over the weekend of September 24 and 25. About 75 cars, including Escort RS2000s, an MGB GT V8 and a heavily modified 1,650cc 100E Popular, were entered and

A typically spirited drive in the Hexagon of Highgate-entered Lister-Jaguar earned Gerry Marshall the honour of winning the very last motor race to be staged at Crystal Palace, the Aston Martin Owner's Club's Historic Sports Car race.

the stage took in part of the old circuit as well as some unmetalled tracks in the park.

Much more widely publicized was the visit of the Autoglass Tour of Britain in September 1989. The Tour of Britain had first been run during the mid-1970s, combining rally stages and circuit racing, and it had attracted large entries and some of the top names in both rallying and racing. The inaugural event in 1973 had been won by James Hunt in a Chevrolet Camaro before the rallymen, Roger Clark, Tony Pond and Ari Vatanen, took over for the next three years. The 1989 revival was an ambitious attempt to recreate the Tour, with a 2,100-mile route starting from the Cardington airship base in Bedfordshire, winding through England and Wales, crossing the sea to Ireland and returning to Scotland, and visiting most racing circuits before the finish at Brands Hatch. The penultimate test was to be a rally stage at Crystal Palace. Unfortunately the project largely failed to fire the imagination of the motor sport world and a disappointing entry of 35 cars dwindled to a meagre 25 starters. The high costs involved in taking part in what was a one-off event were blamed: sponsors and privateers were much more interested in a series of races or rallies, preferably with a championship structure.

Nevertheless there were some highly competitive entries, and most people expected a victor to emerge from the rally drivers, best known of whom were Jimmy McRae and David Llewellin in Ford Sierra RS Cosworths. Derek Bell, five times Le Mans winner and a racer of Formula 3 and 2 cars at the Palace during the 1960s and '70s, was to drive a Vauxhall Astra. At the very last moment, with literally only hours to spare, Roger Clark was tempted out of retirement to compete in a Sierra Cosworth.

The Crystal Palace stage used little of the old circuit. The cars started in the Park and crossed New Link before following the winding prewar track past the Intermediate Lake, arriving at the end of the old top straight and using a couple of hundred yards of the approach to North Tower Crescent. Here they took a sharp left hairpin onto a gravel track, climbed to the loose surface of the former terraces and finished in the old car park. A fairly sparse crowd arrived and were treated to the unlikely sight of a highly modified JCB excavator pulling wheelies along the remains of the top straight before the competitors arrived. Jimmy McRae was by this time holding a comfortable lead which he would maintain to the finish, but Roger Clark was clearly demonstrating that he had lost none of his old skill and proceeded to set fastest time on the stage. Derek Bell walked the stage prior to his run, perhaps remembering his earlier visits to the Palace. David Llewellin, already behind after many problems, had trouble with the Sierra's differential, and would probably want to forget the whole event. The legality of McRae's car was subsequently the subject of a protest by second-place man David Gillanders.

It was all a far cry from the old days of Bira and Mays, Surtees and Salvadori or Rees and Rindt, but perhaps if Crystal Palace can host future events such as this, then the part the circuit played in motor sporting history is more likely to be remembered. For other sports, of course, it continues to be well known. Crystal Palace still holds large-scale athletics events, often seen on TV, and the sports centre continues to provide a whole range of facilities for many sport enthusiasts.

In 1991, if you drive down Anerley Hill from Crystal Palace Parade and turn into Ledrington Road, a sign welcomes you to Crystal Palace National Sports and Recreation Centre. Going in through the gate and towards the car park, anyone who knew the old circuit will suddenly find the look of the place familiar. The old, spacious gravel paddock seems hardly to have changed – even the old corrugated scrutineers' shed is still there, nowadays used as a store. The incline from the paddock to the pits is still intact and if you stand there a while you can almost see the cars assembling for the Formula 2 final! At the top, though, things have changed. The pits have gone, along with the whole of the old Terrace Straight, buried under the earth from the flattened spectator embankments. All around the

A final reminder of Crystal Palace's earlier years is provided as Andy McLennan just manages to hold the tail slide of his enthusiastically driven MGN while under pressure from a Riley and a T-series MG.

Not quite back to path racing, but in 1989 Crystal Palace provided one of the special stages for the 2,100-miles Autoglass Tour of Britain. This is Jimmy McRae laying a dust and smoke cloud in his Ford Sierra with which he dominated the event.

Derek Bell, Britain's foremost sportscar endurance racer, is always happy to have a go at something different and was enticed on to the Autoglass event at the wheel of this Vauxhall Astra.

circuit the familiar whitewashed railway sleeper barriers have been removed and the grass slopes down to the trackside. As you walk towards North Tower Crescent the track reappears from beneath its grassy covering and the tricky corner which saw so many incidents looks much as it did in its final form. Down through the Glade, the rhododendron bushes and trees are as beautiful as ever, encroaching onto the track rather more, but this part of the circuit is pretty much unchanged. Nowadays people walking dogs have replaced the roar of racing machinery. Walk down Park Curve and the New Link drops away below you, or turn right at Fisherman's Bend and follow the prewar track as it twists through the trees past the Intermediate Lake, where the anglers patiently sit, up Fisherman's Rise, passing the Maze and Concert Bowl to Pond Hairpin. On the approach to Big Tree Bend there are a number of tree stumps – perhaps one of them is the tree that gave the corner its name. The road then disappears as New Zealand Hill, Stadium Dip and Cascades Bank have been swallowed up by the sports centre. Back on the postwar circuit, the New Link passes the site of the original start line and the grandstand, where the concrete retaining wall still stands, crumbling and with the white line almost faded from view, but still bearing the scars left by those who failed to make the corner. To the right of the bottom straight is now the swimming pool and in front of that is a track for radio-controlled racing cars, the drivers of which use a platform on the old straight itself – in this miniature way motor racing still thrives at the Palace! Near Ramp Bend the vast Jubilee Stand built in 1977 encroaches on the old track, giving present-day spectators an excellent view of the athletics stadium, once the site of the speedway track and later the paddock of the 1950s. The concrete wall at Ramp Bend stands crumbling and it is still possible to pick out a faded Dunlop advertisement painted on the unforgiving barrier. Climbing Anerley Ramp and Maxim Rise, still recognizable apart from the occasional 'sleeping policeman' to stop people using the service road as the race track it once was, you cross the Ledrington Road entrance and arrive at South Tower Corner, where the barriers have long gone and the old spectator bank slopes down to the edge of the tarmac, which is cracked and pot-holed.

It is sad to see the old circuit like this, but it seems likely much of it will remain in use for the sports centre, and it is still the scene of cycle racing. In a world of madly escalating property prices the site could even have disappeared completely under some anonymous development. Instead, its identity seems safer now than for some time. With the demise of the GLC, responsibility for Crystal Palace has passed to Bromley Borough Council and they have embarked on an ambitious programme to restore many of the park's original features. Working alongside them is the Crystal Palace Foundation, a voluntary body dedicated to the site's preservation. A heritage trail has been laid out taking in many of the surviving elements of the old park including the restored maze, various statues, and some garden and water features still to be restored. The Foundation has opened a museum to maintain Palace memories and relics. There are also plans to build a hotel on the site of the Crystal Palace itself, echoing the style of Paxton's masterpiece, an architectural phoenix to emerge from the ashes of 1936.

The door has long been closed on the former scrutineering bay in the Crystal Palace paddock, but the structure has remained in use for many years on less noisy activities. The local residents finally got their way!

A lap of the track today

There have been many changes to the geography of Crystal Palace during the past 20 years, but parts of the former race track remain as a reminder to motor racing enthusiasts of the good times. Burt Roberts took these pictures when he 'walked' the track in the late 1980s. 1: View from the former startline area of the Terrace Straight looking towards North Tower. 2: North Tower Crescent. 3: The exit from North Tower Crescent. 4: The Glade heading towards Park Curve. 5: The descent from Park Curve through New Link towards the prewar start-finish line. 6: Looking back towards the New Link from the former start-finish straight. 7: The approach to Ramp Bend. 8: Ramp Bend. 9: Anerley Ramp, between Ramp Bend and Maxim Rise. 10: Maxim Rise on the approach to South Tower Corner. 11: South Tower Corner. 12: The exit from South Tower Corner on to Terrace Straight, the start-finish part of which has long been grassed over.

APPENDIX

Crystal Palace lap records and race meetings

Outright record – 2-mile circuit

April 24, 1937	Pat Fairfield	ERA	54.59mph
July 17, 1937	Prince Birabongse	ERA	56.47mph
October 9, 1937	Arthur Dobson	ERA	58.63mph
June 25, 1938	Prince Birabongse	ERA	58.63mph
May 20, 1939	Arthur Dobson	ERA	59.41mph
July 4, 1939	Raymond Mays	ERA	60.97mph

Outright record – 1.39-mile circuit

May 25, 1953	Tony Rolt	Connaught	72.73mph
July 11, 1953	Roy Salvadori	Connaught	73.59mph
June 19, 1954	Reg Parnell	Ferrari	74.69mph
August 2, 1954	Reg Parnell	Ferrari	75.82mph
July 30, 1955	Mike Hawthorn	Maserati	78.93mph
May 21, 1956	Stirling Moss	Maserati	79.94mph
June 10, 1957	Jack Brabham	Cooper-Climax	80.19mph
May 25, 1958	Tommy Bridger	Cooper-Climax	82.30mph
	George Wicken	Cooper-Climax	82.30mph
May 18, 1959	Roy Salvadori	Cooper-Climax	82.30mph
May 18, 1959	Graham Hill	Lotus-Climax	83.12mph
May 22, 1961	Roy Salvadori	Cooper-Climax	83.96mph
	Henry Taylor	Lotus-Climax	83.96mph
June 11, 1962	Innes Ireland	Lotus-BRM	87.46mph
June 7, 1965	Denny Hulme	Brabham-Honda	87.79mph
May 29, 1967	Jacky Ickx	Matra-Ford	94.59mph
	Jean-Pierre Beltoise	Matra-Ford	94.59mph
June 3, 1968	Jochen Rindt	Brabham-Ford	96.60mph
May 25, 1970	Jochen Rindt	Lotus-Ford	100.89mph
	Jackie Stewart	Brabham-Ford	100.89mph
May 31, 1971	Tim Schenken	Brabham-Ford	100.89mph
	Ronnie Peterson	March-Ford	100.89mph
	Emerson Fittipaldi	Lotus-Ford	100.89mph
	Jean-Pierre Jaussaud	March-Ford	100.89mph
May 24, 1972	Mike Hailwood	Surtees-Ford	103.39mph

Motorcycle records – 1.39-mile circuit

50cc

August 17, 1957	F Launchberry	Itom	51.80mph
	E Miniham	Astor Special	53.69mph
August 3, 1959	H German	Sheene Special	55.11mph

125cc

August 17, 1957	D Chadwick	MV Augusta	68.17mph
August 4, 1958	M Hailwood	Ducati	68.74mph
July 2, 1960	K Whorlow	MV Augusta	68.74mph

August 7, 1961	R E Rowe	Honda	69.50mph
April 23, 1962	N Surtees	Bultaco	70.28mph
April 15, 1963	G C A Murphy	Bultaco	73.31mph
April 17, 1969	J Ringwood	MZ	73.37mph

200cc

April 19, 1954	M Cann	FB Mondial	62.08mph
April 2, 1956	M P O'Rourke	MV Augusta	66.72mph
October 6, 1956	C Sandford	Mondial	67.26mph
August 4, 1958	M Hailwood	Ducati	68.74mph

250cc

June 27, 1953	M Cann	Moto Guzzi	66.90mph
April 11, 1954	J Surtees	REG	69.31mph
April 11, 1955	J Surtees	NSU	69.31mph
June 18, 1955	J Surtees	NSU	69.89mph
April 2, 1956	J Surtees	MV Augusta	72.10mph
October 6, 1956	R MacIntyre	Norton	72.10mph
August 17, 1957	J Surtees	NSU	74.24mph
August 5, 1963	P J Dunphy	Greeves	74.46mph
August 30, 1965	R J Everett	Yamaha	76.51mph
April 15, 1968	I Goddard	Yamaha	76.98mph
September 1, 1969	P A Smart	Yamaha	78.43mph
August 31, 1970	P A Smart	Yamaha	80.71mph

350cc

August 22, 1953	M O'Rourke	AJS	69.99mph
April 19, 1954	J Surtees	Norton	71.69mph
April 11, 1955	J Surtees	Norton	72.31mph
October 6, 1956	T S Shepherd	Norton	76.20mph
August 17, 1957	J Surtees	Norton	76.51mph
July 2, 1960	T Thorp	AJS	76.98mph
April 23, 1962	E Minihan	Norton	76.98mph
August 30, 1965	J Blanchard	Norton	77.40mph
April 7, 1969	M Andrew	Kuhn Seeley	77.70mph
August 31, 1970	P A Smart	Yamaha	79.94mph
April 12, 1971	B Ditchburn	Broad Yamaha	79.94mph
April 3, 1972	B Ditchburn	Broad Yamaha	80.50mph

500cc

June 27, 1953	R Keeler	Norton	71.49mph
April 19, 1954	J Surtees	Norton	74.69mph
April 11, 1955	J Surtees	Norton	75.82mph
October 6, 1956	T S Shepherd	Norton	77.94mph
August 17, 1957	J Surtees	Norton	79.43mph
April 23, 1962	P J Dunphy	Norton	79.43mph
April 15, 1963	P J Dunphy	Norton	79.68mph
August 5, 1963	P J Dunphy	Norton	80.19mph

| September 1, 1969 | R Chandler | Seeley | 80.19mph |
| August 31, 1970 | P Mahoney | Kuhn Seeley | 81.50mph |

1,000cc

April 15, 1968	P A Smart	Curley Norton	80.45mph
September 1, 1969	C W Sandby	Kuhn Commando	81.23mph
	P A Smart	Seeley	81.23mph
August 31, 1970	M Ashwood	Weslake Metisse	83.16mph
September 4, 1971	P A Smart	Triumph	84.53mph
August 28, 1972	D Nixon	Boyer Triumph	84.53mph

1,000cc Production Bikes

| August 31, 1970 | R Pickrell | Dunstall Commando | 80.19mph |
| September 4, 1971 | P Williams | Norton Commando | 80.97mph |

Vintage Solo Machines

August 3, 1959	C J Williams	1926 Scott	67.62mph
August 5, 1963	C J Williams	1926 Scott	72.10mph
August 30, 1965	C J Williams	1926 Scott	72.52mph
April 12, 1971	M J Broom	1938 Triumph	72.73mph

Three-Wheelers

August 22, 1953	P Harris	Norton	64.65mph
April 19, 1954	C Smith	Norton	65.84mph
April 11, 1955	W G Boddice	Norton Watsonian	66.19mph
June 18, 1955	W G Boddice	Norton Watsonian	66.72mph
April 2, 1956	A Young	Norton	68.17mph
October 6, 1956	P Harris	Norton	72.73mph
August 3, 1959	E T Young	ETY Triumph	72.73mph
August 3, 1964	T Vinnicombe	Triumph	73.10mph
August 28, 1967	G Boret	Vincent	73.59mph
	P Hardcastle	PJH Triumph	73.59mph
April 15, 1968	C Vincent	BSA Watsonian	75.59mph
April 7, 1969	C Vincent	BSA Watsonian	76.51mph
April 12, 1971	P Brown	BSA	76.98mph
September 4, 1971	G Boret	RGM	76.98mph

Crystal Palace race meetings

Cars

April 24, 1937	Coronation Trophy	Road Racing Club
July 17, 1937	London Grand Prix	Road Racing Club
August 14, 1937	Grand Composite Meeting	Road Racing Club
October 9, 1937	Imperial Trophy	Road Racing Club
April 2, 1938	Coronation Trophy	Road Racing Club
May 21, 1938	Grand Composite Meeting	Road Racing Club
June 26, 1938	London Grand Prix	Road Racing Club
August 14, 1938	Crystal Palace Cup	Road Racing Club
October 8, 1938	Imperial Trophy	Road Racing Club
April 15, 1939	Stanley Cup	Frazer Nash BMW & Vintage Car Club
May 20, 1939	Sydenham Trophy	Road Racing Club
July 1, 1939	Crystal Palace Cup	Road Racing Club
August 26, 1939	Imperial Trophy	Road Racing Club
May 25, 1953	Coronation Trophy	BARC
July 11, 1953	Elizabethan Trophy	Half-Litre Club
September 19, 1953	London Trophy	Half-Litre Club
June 18, 1954	Crystal Palace Trophy	BARC
August 2, 1954	BARC Meeting	BARC
September 18, 1954	Redex Trophy	Half-Litre Club
May 30, 1955	London Trophy	BRSCC
July 30, 1955	International Trophy	BARC
May 21, 1956	London Trophy	BRSCC
August 6, 1956	August Trophy	BARC
June 10, 1957	London Trophy	BRSCC
August 5, 1957	BARC Meeting	BARC
May 26, 1958	Crystal Palace Trophy	BARC
July 5, 1958	BRSCC Meeting	BRSCC
May 18, 1959	London Trophy	BRSCC
August 22, 1959	August Trophy	BARC
November 21, 1958	RAC Rally	RAC
June 6, 1960	Crystal Palace Trophy	BARC
May 22, 1961	London Trophy	BRSCC
September 2, 1961	September Trophy	BARC
June 11, 1962	Crystal Palace Trophy	BARC
September 1, 1962	London Trophy	BRSCC
June 3, 1963	Crystal Palace Trophy	BARC
September 7, 1963	London Trophy	BRSCC
May 18, 1964	London Trophy	BARC
June 13, 1964	Jaguar Drivers Club	JDC
September 5, 1964	Anerley & Norbury Trophies	BRSCC
June 7, 1965	London Trophy	BRSCC
July 3, 1965	Jaguar Drivers Club	JDC
July 31, 1965	Bromley Bowl	BARC
May 30, 1966	London Trophy	BARC
July 2, 1966	Holts Trophy	BARC
August 6, 1966	BRSCC Meeting	BRSCC
May 29, 1967	BUA International Trophy	BRSCC
August 5, 1967	BARC Meeting	BARC
September 9, 1967	Holts Trophy	BARC
June 3, 1968	Holts Formula 2 Trophy	BARC
August 3, 1968	Anerley Trophy	BRSCC
September 14, 1968	Holts Trophy	BARC
November 24, 1968	London-Sydney Marathon	Daily/ Sunday Express
May 26, 1969	Greater London Trophy	BRSCC
August 2, 1969	Daily Express Trophy	BARC
September 13, 1969	British Road Services Trophy	BARC
May 25, 1970	Alcoa Britain Internatl Trophy	BARC
June 13, 1970	Clubmans Motor Racing	TEAC
September 12, 1970	Forward Trust Trophy	BARC
October 3, 1970	Daily Express Trophy	BRSCC
October 17, 1970	Players No 6 Kart Racing	BKC
May 31, 1971	Hilton Transport Trophy	BARC
June 18, 1971	Trumps Moto-Pop	BARC
August 7, 1971	Daily Express/Peytoner Trophy	BRSCC
September 11, 1971	Iberia Airlines Trophy	BARC
September 25, 1971	Daily Mirror Historic Meeting	AMOC
October 16, 1971	National Kart Championships	BKC
May 29, 1972	Greater London Trophy	BARC
August 12, 1972	Peytoner Trophy	BRSCC
September 9, 1972	Hexagon Trophy	BARC
September 23, 1972	Daily Mirror Historic Trophy	AMOC
October 21, 1972	National Kart Championships	BKC
September 24/25, 1977	Southern Rally 77	Southern Car Club

Key to clubs: AMOC = Aston Martin Owners Club; BARC = British Automobile Racing Club; BKC = British Kart Club; BRSCC = British Racing and Sports Car Club; JDC = Jaguar Drivers Club; TESAC = Thames Estuary Auto Club.

Motorcycles

May 21, 1927	Path Racing	London Motor Sports
August 6, 1927	Path Racing	London Motor Sports
September 17, 1927	Path Racing	London Motor Sports
March 18, 1928	Path Racing	London Motor Sports
April 22, 1928	Path Racing	London Motor Sports
May 27, 1928	Path Racing	London Motor Sports
July 1, 1928	Path Racing	London Motor Sports
August 5, 1928	Path Racing	London Motor Sports
November 3, 1928	Path Racing	London Motor Sports
November 29, 1928	Path Racing	London Motor Sports
March 16, 1929	Path Racing	London Motor Sports
June 19, 1929	Evening Meeting	London Motor Sports
July 21, 1929	Evening Meeting	London Motor Sports
August xx, 1929	Evening Meeting	London Motor Sports
November 9, 1929	Path Racing	London Motor Sports

1930–33 – London Motor Sports was involved with the Glaziers Speedway Team

October 28, 1933	Path Racing	Streatham & Dist MCC
April 7, 1934	Path Racing	Streatham & Dist MCC
May 12, 1934	Path Racing	Streatham & Dist MCC
July 2, 1934	Path Racing	Streatham & Dist MCC

1936 – Road Racing Circuit under construction

May 15, 1937	Coronation Grand Prix	Road Racing Club

Remaining prewar motorcycle races were run in conjunction with car meetings

June 27, 1953	BEMSEE Meeting	BEMSEE
August 22, 1953	ACU Meeting	ACU
April 19, 1954	ACU Meeting	ACU
July 17, 1954	BEMSEE Meeting	BEMSEE
April 11, 1955	ACU Meeting	ACU
June 18, 1955	BEMSEE Meeting	BEMSEE
April 2, 1956	ACU Meeting	ACU
October 6, 1956	BEMSEE Meeting	BEMSEE
April 22, 1957	ACU Meeting	ACU
May 18, 1957	BEMSEE Club Day	BEMSEE
August 17, 1957	BEMSEE Meeting	BEMSEE
April 7, 1958	ACU Meeting	ACU
August 4, 1958	BEMSEE Meeting	BEMSEE
October 4, 1958	BEMSEE Club Day	BEMSEE
March 30, 1959	ACU Meeting	ACU
August 3, 1959	BEMSEE Meeting	BEMSEE
April 18, 1960	ACU Meeting	ACU

July 2, 1960	Guinness Trophy	BEMSEE
August 1, 1960	BEMSEE Meeting	BEMSEE
April 3, 1961	ACU Meeting	ACU
August 7, 1961	BEMSEE Meeting	BEMSEE
April 23, 1962	ACU Meeting	ACU
August 6, 1962	BEMSEE Meeting	BEMSEE
April 15, 1963	ACU Meeting	ACU
August 3, 1963	BEMSEE Meeting	BEMSEE
March 30, 1964	ACU Meeting	ACU
August 3, 1964	BEMSEE Meeting	BEMSEE
April 19, 1965	ACU Meeting	ACU
August 30, 1965	BEMSEE Meeting	BEMSEE
April 11, 1966	ACU Meeting	ACU
August 29, 1966	BEMSEE Meeting	BEMSEE
March 27, 1967	ACU Meeting	ACU
August 28, 1967	BEMSEE Meeting	BEMSEE
April 15, 1968	ACU Meeting	ACU
September 7, 1968	BEMSEE Meeting	BEMSEE
April 7, 1969	ACU Meeting	ACU
September 1, 1969	BEMSEE Meeting	BEMSEE
March 30, 1970	ACU Meeting	ACU
August 31, 1970	BEMSEE Meeting	BEMSEE
April 12, 1971	ACU Meeting	ACU
September 4, 1971	BEMSEE Meeting	BEMSEE
April 3, 1972	ACU Meeting	ACU
August 28, 1972	BEMSEE Meeting	BEMSEE

Key to clubs: ACU = Auto Cycle Union; BEMSEE = British Motorcycle Racing Club

Crystal Palace Speedway

The Glaziers league positions

1929 Southern League (11 teams): 1st Stamford Bridge (34pts); 4th Crystal Palace (22pts)
1930 Southern League (13 teams): 1st Wembley (41pts); 7th Crystal Palace (23pts)
1931 Southern League (10 teams): 1st Wembley (59 pts); 4th Crystal Palace (44pts)
1932 NPA Trophy Competition (10 teams): 1st Stamford Bridge (32pts); 3rd Crystal Palace (24pts) 1932 National League (9 teams): 1st Wembley (24pts); 2nd Crystal Palace (20pts)
1933 National League (10 teams): 1st Belle Vuw (62pts); 4th Crystal Palace (42pts)
1934 National League (9 teams): 1st Belle Vue (52pts); 3rd *Crystal Palace/New Cross (40pts) *Team moved and changed name mid-season